Puffin Plus
The Boy who saw

All his life Leo had lived behind or above
shops. Mostly milk bars and newsagencies like
the one in the small township of Manoora,
where he had just moved with his mother and
Rick.

Leo tried hard not to hate Rick, his mother's
friend. His mother had told him that being with
Rick made things easier for her. Leo couldn't
understand why – Rick was awful to her, and
deliberately made life difficult for him.

Then when Leo believes that God has ordered
him to sacrifice a sheep, little does he realize the
consequences his action will have . . .

A haunting story by the author of *The Pochetto
Coat* (in Puffin).

The Boy who saw God

Ted Greenwood

PUFFIN BOOKS

Penguin Books Australia Ltd,
487 Maroondah Highway, P.O. Box 257
Ringwood, Victoria, 3134, Australia
Penguin Books Ltd,
Harmondsworth, Middlesex, England
Penguin Books,
625 Madison Avenue, New York, N.Y. 10022, U.S.A.
Penguin Books Canada Ltd,
2801 John Street, Markham, Ontario, Canada
Penguin Books (N.Z.) Ltd,
182-190 Wairau Road, Auckland 10, New Zealand

First published by HUTCHINSON GROUP (Australia) Pty Ltd, 1980
Published by Penguin Books Australia, 1983

Copyright ©Ted Greenwood, 1980

Offset from the Hutchinson edition
Made and printed in Hong Kong by
LP & Associates Ltd

CIP

Greenwood, Ted, 1930-
The boy who saw God

First published: Richmond, Vic.:
Hutchinson of Australia, 1980.
ISBN 0 14 031583 7.

I. Title.

A823'.3

One

'Guess what?'

'What?' shouted a voice from higher up in the cypress.

'I can see my old man going down the back path to our outside dunny.'

'Garn, I bet you can't.'

'Yes I can...he's just gone past the lemon tree and now he's going in and...aw, he's shut the door!'

Laughter shook the greenery near the top of the tree.

'Well from where I am, I can see old Bill Wyatt opening the cemetery gates for someone', called the higher voice.

'I bet it's not a funeral, not on a Saturday.'

'Nup, it's not. It's just a council truck.'

'With a load of bodies, I bet.'

More laughter from the top. Woodoh loved to get laughs from his mates. He and Carl, and sometimes Peter, spent odd Saturdays climbing these trees or just messing about up on Crater Hill.

The way up to the hill passed the cemetery bordered by a long row of close-knit cypresses. If it was too much of a drag to push their bikes all the way to the top for races down again, they could hide them behind the dense greenery that swept close to the ground. And behind this screen, out of the wind, were plenty of good spots to have a pee.

They liked the windy days best for climbing, climbing as high as they were game, hanging out on the springy branches and warbling like magpies. This day, they perched at various heights, spying out in different directions.

Woodoh bounced up and down on his branches to open out his view down to Manoora. Though he often exaggerated what he saw from his perches, it would be possible from where he sat to catch glimpses of their town below, bits like the memorial clock, the racecourse and the river, and even his own backyard.

Carl looked out across the cemetery and over the houses and gardens on that side of town, and beyond to the patchwork of farms, lakes, and roads stretching away to the east.

Peter, the smallest of the three, was never game enough to climb as high as the others. He had only a framed view of a grassy slope on Crater Hill to report on. He couldn't even see the top of the hill that once, aeons ago, had been a volcano, but now stood as a harmless green cone rising from the wind-swept plains. Who'd want to hear about Baldy Braithwaite's dirty sheep grazing their way round the sides of Crater Hill? Nothing funny or new in that.

'It's not bodies, Woodoh', yelled Carl, 'it's just an empty truck'.

'It's come to pick up a load of skeletons then.'

Peter heard, but he didn't join in the laughter

this time. He had caught sight of a figure scrambling through the tussocks on the hill. Something for him to report on.

'Hey!' he called up to the others, 'I just saw a kid up on Crater'.

'So what?' said Carl.

Woodoh showed more interest. 'Who is it?' he asked.

Peter strained out as far as he could to keep the figure in sight. 'Dunno', he said, 'can't tell from this far away, but it's a kid — skinny, kind of red hair I think, could be that new kid — here he comes again, reckon he's chasing something.'

'What's up there to chase?' said Carl.

'I can't see yet, wait a minute. Yes, there it goes — it's one of the sheep; it just ran across the bit I can see, and he went past soon after.'

'What a nut!' Carl scoffed, 'he can't know much about sheep if he thinks just anyone can run after one and grab it, and anyway, who'd want to be catching one of those greasy old things?'

'Can you see him again?' called Woodoh.

'Nup, not now.'

'Well let's go down and see who it is', said Woodoh, already lowering himself to Peter's level, just expecting the other two to follow on down after him.

They did. All three threaded their way down through the network of dry, dusty twigs and branches close to the main trunk. Peter was passed and left behind as the others swung easily down to the ground and then pushed their way out through the greenery into the open.

Yes, Peter had been right, there was a kid up on

Crater Hill, but if he'd been chasing sheep, then he'd given it up, because now he was scrambling down the slope, heading for the bitumen driveway that wound down from the top. All they could see of the sheep were a couple of backs bounding from sight over the ridge of the cone.

'Quick, before he sees us, back in behind the trees', said Woodoh.

By the time Peter joined them, the other two were huddled together in amongst the low branches.

'What's doing?' he asked.

Carl motioned him to keep his voice down and stay beside them.

'He's coming down the road', said Woodoh, 'we'll give him a bit of a scare'.

'Do you reckon it's that new kid?' asked Peter.

'Not positive, but we'll soon find out.'

They stared out, waiting to spot the figure pass. The padding of feet on the bitumen hardly reached them before the runner sped by their hiding-place. Woodoh was a bit late starting his howling animal noises. 'Hey, you!' was all Carl could think to shout out.

The boy stopped a short distance on, turned and scanned the greenery for the source of the shouting and noises. The scare tricks hadn't worked too well.

'Come on', said Woodoh, 'we might as well show ourselves now that you've mucked it up, Carl'.

'Your weak noises wouldn't have scared a flea', grumbled Carl, following Woodoh out into the open.

The figure stood in the middle of the roadway. He was doubled forward, hands gripping knees, body heaving with each panted breath. It was the new kid.

When he straightened up and looked directly at them, they weren't quite ready for that kind of face — papery white, and red eyes, either from the wind or crying. Carl thought it looked a bit like a ghost's. Woodoh thought it looked too old to be on a kid's body. Peter thought it looked weird.

The boy stayed still, staring like a white-faced steer, not turning or attempting to run off.

'What's your name?' asked Carl, when they were standing close to him.

He didn't answer. His head didn't move. Only the eyes, searching each of his challengers in turn.

'Don't you remember, his name's Leo', Peter whispered to Carl, 'Leo Farrell'.

Carl nodded. 'Oh yeah, Leo Farrell, that's your name, isn't it?' he said, stepping closer to the boy.

Still he didn't answer. If he expected arm-twisting or punching, he didn't look scared at all. Just blank.

Woodoh looked at his mates, shrugged his shoulders and made a face, as if to suggest 'this kid's a kook!'

Carl did reach out, grab the boy's pullover at the sleeve, and give it a shake of impatience at his silence. 'What were you doing up on Crater Hill?' he demanded.

Still no answer.

'Listen, we're not going to hurt you', said Woodoh, without menace, 'Peter here says he saw you chasing a sheep up there. If you were, then you're a bit of a nut, because they belong to old man Braithwaite who lives in that first house there just outside the reserve gates, and he'd get stuck into you if he saw you. Did you try to catch one of them?'

The boy seemed more ready to answer Woodoh, even if it was only by a jerky nod of the head.

'Well it's lucky for you that old Braithwaite wasn't at his window or out on the reserve somewhere. He looks after the whole park up here you know, and he's always on the look-out. And anyway, why try to catch one of his greasy old sheep. What's the fun in that?'

The white lips opened. 'I have to', the boy said, huskily.

'What?' said Woodoh, screwing his face in disbelief.

'I have to.'

'Why?' asked Carl.

'Because . . . because . . .'

'Because what?' demanded Woodoh.

'Because . . . God wants me to!' It was almost a relief for him to get it out, however softly.

'Who wants you to?' asked Carl, who wasn't sure if he'd heard correctly.

The extra question was one too many for the boy. He stepped away, then turned and fled.

Carl started to chase after him, but Woodoh took only a few steps, calling, 'Hey! Who wants you to?'

But there was no turning back, and the boy sprinted down through the reserve gateway and into the street beyond. Carl gave up the chase

10

when he realized his friends were not bothering.

'That kid really is a nut!' he said, when he joined them again.

'Did you hear what he said?' asked Woodoh.

'Nup, not really, his voice sounded funny and croaky.'

'He said God wanted him to catch the sheep', Peter said, quietly.

'God?' Carl couldn't believe it.

'That's what I thought he said', Woodoh nodded.

'Now that really is crazy', said Carl, 'he must be joking to say that God told him to catch a sheep'.

'Yeah', laughed Woodoh, 'who does he think he's kidding? Fancy saying that to old Braithwaite if he caught you! Come on, let's go and get our bikes from under the trees.'

Peter said nothing. And he said nothing when the other two kept laughing about the new kid and his sheep-chasing for God.

But he thought about it a lot.

Two

Leo wasn't running now. He walked along the Manoora main street, head down, scuffing his heels on the pavement. He nearly went right past the milk bar. A couple of billboards blown over by the wind stopped him. He picked them up and propped them against the shop front without thinking.

Always shops. Leo had lived all his life behind or above shops. Mostly milk bars and newsagencies like this one in Manoora. It looked a bit older than the last one down in the city, but it had the same jumble of signs and boards out front, peeling white paint around the window, and the same stuff in the window, like bread, a few cakes, stacks of tins, and cartons. This was home; there was nowhere else for him to go.

Raised voices reached him from inside — that meant only one thing. Rick was having a go at Leo's mother and she was trying to argue back. There wouldn't be any customers inside, then.

Leo stood at the door for a moment, listening to the voices, hearing enough to know that Rick was complaining about him. He thought of waiting until a customer came along before going in himself. They'd have to stop their arguing then. But he didn't get the chance. Rick must have caught sight of him loitering outside. Without warning, the door was flung open, Rick grabbed him by the arm and hauled him into the shop.

'Where have you been, then?' he demanded.

'Just out', said Leo.

'It's always "just out" isn't it? You know well enough that we can do with your help around the shop on Saturdays, and yet you just piss off without saying a word.'

'Rick, please.'

That was all his mother ever said when Rick used words like that. Leo knew she would never swear back at Rick. She had told Leo many times that it wasn't right in the sight of God.

Rick propelled him further into the shop, then held him in one spot by the collar with his strong, pudgy hand. 'As I've said before Nola, your precious only chick is hopeless, bloody hopeless.'

Leo didn't bother to fight against Rick's grasp — he'd learnt long before that struggling against him was useless, and his mother had only her words to use in his defence. How could her sparse frame, the thin arms and gentle, bony fingers restrain someone as solid as Rick?

'You expect too much from him, Rick', she said, 'he's only eleven, remember. Can't you remember what you were like at eleven?'

'A bloody sight more useful than this.'

Leo was saved from any more of this by the appearance of a customer. It gave him the chance to escape. He moved quickly away from Rick, went through an opening between the counters, past

13

his mother who reached out to touch his arm as he went by, giving him a quick, reassuring smile. But without turning to her, Leo went out through the door leading to the rooms they lived in. In his haste, he knocked against the stacks of crates holding empty milk and soft drink bottles that cluttered up the passageway at the foot of the stairs leading up to the rooms above the shop. They rattled dangerously, and he had to stop and grab one that was knocked askew. Anxiously, he quickly shoved it back into its place. Rick would have shouted at him for this too, but although Leo couldn't see Rick's face, he knew that now he would be wearing his shop smile. The round, red face could look quite friendly and jolly when it wanted to — polished and as shiny as the tight curly hair on top.

'Is Manoora always as cold and windy as this?' Leo heard him asking the customer in his weather-talk, shop voice.

Leo had heard them all. Rick had a 'chase the animals from in front of the shop' voice. He had an 'order Leo's mother about' voice, a 'man customer' voice, a 'lady customer' voice, a 'girl customer' voice, and even different ones for kids and old people.

As Leo climbed the dark stairs, Rick's voice in the shop faded away, and when he closed his bedroom door, Leo shut it out altogether as so often he had done in other rooms behind or above other shops. There, he could be alone with his thoughts or his dioramas.

He'd copied the first diorama from an old hobbies book which he'd found in the library of a school he had attended back in the city.

You could make up any scenes you wanted, build them out of bits and pieces, and set them up inside a box. And when holes were cut in the lid of the box and then covered with coloured cellophanes, the light shone down on the little models inside. If it was a long box and the peep-hole was at one end, then the scene inside looked as though it went on for ages and ages into the distance, just like some he'd seen once in a museum. You could make everything multiply if you placed mirrors inside — one house made of matchboxes could be made to look like a whole street of houses all the same.

The Bible stories made the best dioramas. Daniel really looked as though he was in a lion's den, with all that straw on the floor of the box. And with just a couple of light-holes cut out close together, it made the light shine down as into a prison-cell from a tiny window. The light just touched him kneeling there surrounded by paper lions. And the paper flames twirling up around Shadrach, Meshach, and Abednego looked redder and hotter if the light-holes were held close under Leo's bed-lamp.

His Noah's Ark diorama was his favourite. He had used the biggest box he could find from the shop for this one. The Ark had taken ages to make, with all those ice-cream sticks and matches covering the sides of the boat, and the painted glass on the bottom of the box made a smooth, shiny stretch of water to place it on. The best thing about this diorama was that you could think of more and more animals to make. All the decks

15

and the roof of the Ark were crowded, but he always seemed to find room for another pair, and if they fell off, well, that must have happened sometimes with the real Ark, Leo was sure of that. He had made a couple of animal heads and sat them on the glass to look like stragglers swimming after the Ark. And he'd hung a big, coloured, cotton-wool cloud from the lid, but he hadn't tried to make any raindrops. He wanted it to look as though the sun had just peeped through from behind a cloud.

Leo didn't get out his dioramas this time. He just sprawled on his bed and stared out through the one window which faced the backyards of the adjoining shops. Nothing much to look at out there, but he didn't mind. It was a good nothing-view to gaze at while he thought about catching that sheep for God. He was sure that was what God had meant up on the hill that those kids had called Crater.

God had spoken to him before, down in the city, but this was the first time he had really shown himself. The light had dazzled Leo for a moment or two, but it was God right enough, sitting in a ray of light that stabbed out from the clouds. Leo hadn't answered, but he was positive that the figure had pointed to the sheep. And sheep are very important in the Bible.

Leo knew all about the story of Abraham and the burnt offering. And he remembered that Abraham wasn't the only one in the Bible to offer a sheep to God as a sacrifice. Why would God want Leo to do it too? He wasn't a man like Abraham, so why had God asked him to do it?

For as long as Leo could remember, his mother always said not to ask too many questions. Not about the Bible stories she used to read to him from that fat book with pictures in it, or what the sermon meant at Church, or even about his real father.

'Just accept it', she'd say, smiling her pale smile.

And that's what she'd always said if Leo told her he didn't want her to stay with Rick any more. Then she would clasp him by the arms and make him face her, looking into his eyes as if searching for something, blue eyes to blue eyes, hers the first to flicker and turn away, and she'd say, 'Don't Leo, don't talk like that. Let's make the best of it all — together.'

Leo tried hard not to hate Rick. His mother told him that the Bible said you shouldn't hate. She knew a lot about the Bible, and yet she wanted to live with Rick, who could be awful. Leo had never seen Rick kiss his mother, but he supposed he must, some time when he wasn't around.

His mother told him that being with Rick made things easier for her. Leo tried to understand how that could be. Perhaps it was because she didn't have to run about as much any more, yet she seemed to be always saying she was tired now. Leo remembered she used to smile more — a tall, smiling mother, a pink face edged with wispy hair, a whiff of some sweet smell when the soft cheek pressed against his as she said goodnight. Her gold hair used to be tied in two bunches like a girl's. They bounced when she ran about — always running, that was it. Backwards and forwards from the shop and the rooms at the back,

back to his father sitting there, staring. Leo could remember the stare and the smile and the rug covering the knees, but not the rest, not any of the words.

Yet he often wished his real father hadn't gone. It was best for his father to die — that's what his mother told him if ever Leo said he wished him back again. God would look after Leo, she'd say; God was his father.

Well now he had shown himself, and Leo was going to do what God wanted, just in case he grew angry with him and left him again with only Rick for a father.

Those boys who had stopped him said he would get into trouble from someone called Braithwaite if he caught one of those sheep up on the hill, but that wouldn't matter because God would look after him. The only trouble was that God hadn't told him how to catch the sheep in the first place. Up there on the hill was the first time he had ever been near a sheep, and it wasn't like trying to catch a cat or a dog, the only other animals he'd had anything to do with before.

It wouldn't be easy, but he would go up to the hill over and over again until he found a way. He remembered that Abraham had found a sheep stuck by its horns in a bush, but there was only grass up on that hill, and none of the sheep he saw up there had horns, so he'd have to work out a way to trap one.

'Leo!'

Rick's voice blocked out any plans for a sheep trap. It didn't pay to pretend he hadn't heard whenever Rick shouted like that, so Leo left his thoughts with his dioramas, and went downstairs.

From the foot of the stairs, he could see his mother back in the kitchen, but escape into there with her wasn't possible — Rick saw him first and called him into the shop.

'Right, dopey, make yourself useful and bring in the papers from the street — they've just arrived', he ordered.

Without answering him, Leo obediently went out, picked up one of the bundles by the binding and struggled back inside, the twine cutting into his fingers, the bundle banging against his spindly shins.

'Here, cut them open with this.'

Rick threw across a long, pointed knife. Leo started, and jumped to avoid its point as it bounced off the bundle near his hand. He retrieved it, knelt down beside the bundle, and began to saw through the taut twine. It slackened and fell from the bundle, but instead of pulling it out from under the newspapers, Leo stayed kneeling, gazing at the rope-end in his hand.

Rick caught sight of him propping there. 'Come on, bring those papers up on to the counter, no one's going to buy them down there on the floor, and don't go off to sleep again and forget there's another bundle still outside.'

Leo did as he was told, still clutching the knife and the twine. After the second bundle had been cut open and the papers arranged on the counter, he picked up the lengths of twine and wound them round from elbow to hand in a neat hank. Leo knew that now he must try to claim these pieces of twine.

'Could I have this rope?' he asked, not looking directly at Rick in case the heavy-lidded but sharp eyes searched his face and discovered just how keen he was to have it, and then that would have been the end of it.

He always had to ask for anything from the shop, even waste like this rope. Sometimes his mother let him serve himself with a can of drink or an ice-cream, but he couldn't get away with even a stale chocolate or a torn magazine with Rick. He was luckier this time. Rick hardly glanced up from the newspaper headlines. 'Yeah, so long as you don't hang yourself with it', he said.

And no questions why.

Three

Getting the rope was one thing. Getting back up to Crater Hill the next day was another. Sundays for Leo often were filled up. First by his mother with church in the morning, and then by Rick who always tried to find extra jobs for him in the afternoon.

Rick didn't attempt to stop them going to church together, but he'd often make fun of her as she and Leo left the shop. 'All dolled-up for the boss up there, Nola?' he'd say, pointing up, or, 'Say a prayer for a poor bloody sinner like me who has to work, won't you.'

A different crack each time — about religion, God, or about Leo's mother and the little extra care she took getting ready for church, brushing some lustre into her lank hair, gathering the loose ends away from her face, bringing back the smooth cheeks and some of the pink glow with make-up, making the outing seem special with a touch of perfume — more for Leo than for the Lord. Leo noticed it all, but these days he kept his affection hidden. He asked her once why they kept going to church when Rick made such fun of it.

'It's something that's in my blood Leo — mine, and yours too', she told him, 'and that means we shouldn't give it up just because others don't see anything in it. It's something we can hang on to, something that's always the same. We need it to help us cope with everything.'

Church-time this Sunday was close before anyone came to get Leo out of bed.

'You get your own breakfast, Leo!' shouted Rick, banging on the door, 'Your mother doesn't want to get out of bed this morning.'

Leo lay listening to the heavy footsteps clomping down the stairs. Strange that on this particular morning, he might be missing church. A disappointing thought at first.

Church might be different for him now, after seeing God like that. It might be much more than standing there during prayers, peering furtively at everyone and imagining what they were thinking and seeing; more than watching his mother fumble in her bag for her handkerchief and dab the tears away during the Benediction. Yes, it might be quite different, now.

In all the times he had been taken to church, he had never seen anything like God. He had tried and tried to find something in the light that sometimes streamed in through the windows, but nothing ever appeared. And when they said the name over and over, you'd think God would be easy to see, but he wasn't. Now, Leo would know what to expect.

But then perhaps it was better not to be going to church today. It would make it easier to finish his shop chores early, and then maybe slip away with the rope up to the hill. Getting that sheep for God was more important than seeing him in church, so why not try again today?

He went to his mother's room first. She was lying in bed, her face pinched by migraine, her pallor almost a match for the pillow.

'Aren't we going today?' asked Leo from the door.

Her eyes moved, but not her head. 'No Leo, I don't feel very well this morning.'

'Will I have to help in the shop?'

'You'll have to ask Rick.'

Leo knew that's what she would say. She was content now to let Rick give the orders around the shop. More and more now she worked in the rooms and let him run everything.

Leo didn't have to ask Rick for jobs. He was called even before he'd finished his breakfast.

'Spring off your bum and get those crates out of the passage and into the backyard', was Rick's second order for the day.

They came one after the other like that for the rest of the morning. Clean down the bloody ice-cream cabinet. Fill the bloody drink-fridge. Wipe over the bloody floor of the shop. Odds and ends until the Sunday papers came in.

But Leo didn't forget about God. He didn't wait for any more orders after lunch. He took his mother a snack.

'Are you getting on all right down there, love?' she asked.

Leo nodded, then quickly retreated before any awkward questions came up.

It pained Leo's mother to watch him disappear

as quickly as he had come. No hugs these days — just a nod and then away. Not even holding hands on the way to church. No good blaming Rick for that, she thought.

No good going back. Rick was here to stay, but she wished he could be softer with Leo, that's what he needed, not all that pushing about. Yet things might have been worse if he hadn't dropped in that day, helped her clean up the stock and the books, and then stayed. It seemed all for the best at the time, but — no good going over and over it. She wasn't up to thinking clearly or even praying about it, not right then.

Leo went straight to his room and pulled out the length of twine he had hidden under his bed. He tried to stuff it under his jacket, but he thought he mightn't get past Rick looking like that. It was too fat a hank to put into a pocket so, starting at the ankle, he wound it round and round his leg all the way up and above the knee. His jeans pulled down over it, but it felt stiff when he started to walk down the stairs.

Along the passage from the foot of the stairs, he could see Rick's broad frame leaning over the counter, probably with a paper spread out. Leo slipped into the kitchen. He stood in the room, not quite sure why he was there. It wasn't just the fear of Rick seeing him, he must have needed something — matches, yes, that was it. He might need matches if he was to make a burnt offering. Abraham wouldn't have used matches. They made fire in other ways, then.

He didn't take the used box from beside the stove — someone might notice it missing. New packets were always kept in one of the high cup-boards. Would God keep Rick in the shop? Leo took a chance and climbed on a chair to reach the matches. The cupboard door made what seemed to him a loud click. Leo froze, his hand on the handle, listening. Surely God wouldn't let him be discovered, not right at the beginning.

He didn't. And the chair was quietly put back and the matches safely concealed in a pocket of his jeans.

Leo felt there was something else he needed to look for in the kitchen as well. It was something to do with the twine — when he took it off the news-papers — that pointy knife that Rick had thrown.

A knife! Couldn't use a knife! The thought shocked him. But it wouldn't be right to burn it alive. Perhaps that's what they did, though — burnt them alive.

It would have to be one of the kitchen knives, not the one in the shop. One of those peeling knives in the cutlery drawer, that would do, they had sharp points and sharp blades. Leo poked the knife down inside the rope below the calf of his leg, safe against discovery, but not too safe for his skin.

Though he felt God would be helping, Leo couldn't bring himself to go out through the shop, past Rick. Imagine the trouble if that knife fell from its hiding-place just as he was going through the shop! Rick would be right on to him, then. No, he wouldn't be risking that. He slipped out through the backyard.

As he walked through the town, he kept expecting someone to stop him and ask him where he was going, but there were hardly any people about at that time on a Sunday, and none of those he passed took any notice of him at all. As he approached the entrance to the Crater Hill reserve, he remembered the warnings those boys had given him about the man they called Baldy Braithwaite. What if he was in his front garden now?

But he wouldn't stop you going into the reserve. It had a notice saying it was a public park. He couldn't stop you.

Leo sped up a little as he passed Braithwaite's house. If the man was there in the garden, then Leo couldn't see him because of the hedge. The best way is to go straight on without looking back. Anyway, God wasn't going to let anyone stop him.

Leo did feel that he was being watched. It made him turn around once or twice, but nobody was in sight, and nobody called out to him. And his spirits rose when he looked up to the hill and saw a number of sheep moving slowly around its sides.

Where the road curved sharply to skirt the hill, Leo left it and headed up the steeper slope through the grass. The message of his deliberate approach reached the sheep, and some huddled closer together. Others took a few nervous bounds towards the ridge.

Leo stopped, sat down, pulled up the leg of his jeans and began to unravel the rope. The little flock calmed again and returned to their more relaxed cropping, but he kept watching them to see if he should speed up the unravelling.

More than pressure from the rope had marked

his leg — dried blood followed a rope pattern starting from where the point of the knife had pierced his skin . . . There would be more blood running from the sheep when he caught it. It would get mixed up with the wool. Leo tried to put off thinking about that.

Carefully, he put the knife into a side-pocket, handle first, hoping to save the lining and his thigh from its sharp point. The rope looked much shorter up here than it had looked in the bedroom where it had stretched from one wall to the other and half-way back again, and the loop looked smaller too. A sheep's head might just fit through it, but not a sheep with horns.

Nearly all the sheep had worked their way up near to the ridge when Leo started after them again. He moved forward very slowly up the slope, pausing after every pace, trying to fool the sheep into thinking he was a pole or a thin stump sticking out of the ground. Leo had seen cats crawling one careful step at a time nearer and nearer to their prey like that. He wished he could have crawled on all fours and still held the rope at the ready. One silly sheep was further behind than the others, but it shouldn't matter to God what sort of sheep it was for the sacrifice, silly, or smart like the one leading the others over the hill.

Even if he had been very close, Leo's first cast of the rope wouldn't have looped over anything more than a tussock of grass. All it did was to wake up the slow sheep and it bounded away to join the rest on their way over the bare ridge where, one after the other, they showed out clearly against the pale cloudy sky before disappearing from sight.

'Hey you up there! What are you doing with those sheep?'

Leo heard the 'Hey you' part of the shouting, but the rest was just a gabble of words to him from that far away. He turned quickly and looked back down the reserve. What he saw made him scramble away as fast as he could to the top of the hill.

It was the wrong thing to do. It made Braithwaite suspicious enough to come up after him.

'What does that bloody stupid kid think he's playing at with my sheep?' he grumbled out loud as he pushed his big frame forward as fast as he could.

Leo kept scrambling and falling over tussocks in his haste to reach the top, and the loose rope kept getting in the way. He tripped over it, and as he fell, his hand brushed the point of the knife sticking out of his jeans. The cut was neat but it was painful. His sharp cry was stifled by his rapid breathing. There was no time for sucking or dabbing. He just left it to throb and ooze as he picked himself up and went on, trailing the rope behind him. When he reached the ridge, he turned back to see if the man was still coming up after him. Yes, he was still in pursuit, though he hadn't gained much.

Turning away from the man struggling up through the grass, Leo looked for escape. The rim of Crater Hill curved away from him in a perfect circle, enclosing the ancient mouth of the volcano, now a deep but docile bowl of grass with only protruding stones or an occasional prickly hawthorn-bush offering any sort of hiding-place. All the sheep were working their way down to the base of the crater. Leo took one further panicky look back at his pursuer. Either run around the rim or try to hide down in the crater — only two possibilities he could see for escape. He chose to hide.

It was even worse running down the inner slopes of Crater Hill. The grass and the stones together made the going more uneven than the tussocks on the outside of the hill, and while the ground had looked smooth and even from up on the rim, there were many hollows hidden by the grass. He tripped and pitched into one of these, and though his hands and knees were jarred by the fall, he quickly crawled back behind the thick grass growing on the edge of the hollow. This gave him cover from anyone standing on the rim of the hill directly above his hiding-place.

Leo watched with apprehension as the sheep made another of their rushes up the other side of the bowl directly opposite him, but thankfully the steepness of the slope and his disappearance calmed their charge, and soon they stopped altogether.

Through a grass filter, he kept watch on the rim for what seemed ages until the figure appeared. It looked huge and black, as clean a silhouette as the sheep had been. It stood with legs apart, and though he couldn't see the face clearly, Leo could tell by the movement of the man that the eyes were searching the inside of the bowl. If he decided to come down the slope, then nothing would save Leo from discovery. If the man decided to walk around the rim to the opposite side, it would be just as bad — Leo would be easy to spot from there.

Braithwaite was panting too much from the effort of climbing to be keen about continuing the chase. His sheep looked O.K. to him, and though he couldn't count them one by one from where he stood, he was fairly sure they were all there, and that they wouldn't stray far.

'Why should the little bugger want to rope one of the sheep? Boys do some damn fool things at times. It'd have to be one of the town kids; none of the farm kids would do it, that's for sure.'

Braithwaite stood there until his puffing subsided. For one awful moment, Leo thought he was going to come down into the bowl, but he only took enough steps to get down out of the wind to light a cigarette.

Now that Leo could see the figure more clearly, he could tell that the man really had a big bald head, and the arms he held up as he lit his cigarette looked big, too. Rick was small compared to that. Imagine what this one could do if he got hold of you!

Leo still thought that God would stop the man coming any further, but he was fearful about it, just the same. He kept as still as he could, even though his cut hand was burning and his knees tucked up were hurting from his fall.

He didn't move when Braithwaite turned and went back up to the rim. Just as well for him that he didn't, because the big man stood there again for a moment, giving the bowl a last look for any sign of movement.

Not until the dark statue came to life again

and disappeared from sight did Leo dare even to stretch out his legs, but he kept the rest of his body hidden in the hollow for quite a time after that, God or no God.

Four

Leo couldn't hold back tears. Through his own mist he looked across at the sheep calmly grazing on the opposite side of the bowl as if no one had ever interrupted their feeding. They know I'm here though, he was sure of that.

A darkening sky didn't help. The afternoon seemed to be closing fast without anything to show for all his effort. And probably Rick had missed him by now. So why not have one more try? It wouldn't make any difference. Rick would lay into him, not just a shaking this time, especially if his mother was still in bed and out of the way. He started to edge forward, a kind of baby shuffle, legs pushed out straight, then bend knee and bring the bottom up, straighten out legs again, bend the knees and bring the bottom back up again.

Whenever any of the sheep on the other side looked up, Leo froze. But it worked. The sheep moved only slowly around the bowl rather than up, allowing Leo to come much closer than he had managed to do on the outside of the crater. But he would have to choose the right moment to stand up and run. A bigger boulder gave him some cover. Slowly he pulled out the rope again and got to his feet.

'Now I'll get one for you, God!'

Leo jumped out, ran down the last part of the slope, through a tumble of boulders sitting amongst the grass at the base of the bowl, and scrambled up the opposite side. The sheep scattered wildly away from him. God wasn't going to help him then.

His eyes stung with frustrated tears again, but just as he was about to give up, one of the slowest and fattest sheep fell. It let out a pathetic cry as it struggled to wrench its leg free from the hole that had brought about its downfall. Leo flung himself forward towards it. The sheep was almost on its back now, floundering and flailing its free hoofs, hoofs which Leo foolishly ignored in his triumph.

Even his light body dropping on it made the sheep baa again like a cry from a pressed doll. But its hoofs found their mark over and over again as Leo desperately tried to tie a pair of them together. The pain of the blows made him cry out too, and in the struggle, he almost missed seeing the knife which had dropped to the ground and nearly disappeared under the rolling body of the sheep. Leo gave up trying to rope it, but kept holding on to one of the jerking legs, and with the other hand, he grabbed the knife.

For his size, he went mad with it. Not looking, or caring about his own soreness, or where he was striking, he stabbed again and again. Despite the flurry of blows, few of Leo's stabs penetrated the thick wool. He didn't pause until one blow hit on a hard, bony spot, jarring his hand. The knife dropped and he shook his wrist in pain. He was forced to let go of the leg held with his other hand, but surprisingly the sheep didn't keep struggling or jerking beneath him now. Leo could hear its heaving breath, and the one eye he could see rolled wildly, but its body was still.

The smell of it, the pain in his wrist, and the sight of blood seeping through the wool, widening out into dirty red stains, turned Leo's stomach and he dry-retched.

A quiver from the body beneath him was a warning that at any moment the sheep might renew its violent struggling and escape. He had little trouble this time securing two legs with the rope, and then he ran the end of it across and tied it to a third leg that waved within his reach.

Only then did he rise from the sheep, but he picked up the knife again just in case. He crouched by its side, listening for the panted breathing to stop, looking anywhere but at the sheep and its bloodied wool.

Not alive, I couldn't burn it alive. He looked up to the sky for another shaft of light, another sight of God, but the greyness shifting over Crater Hill didn't break.

I can't wait for it to die, it could be dark by then. He turned back to the sheep, still safely trussed, still lying where it had fallen. It's lying still — I can stick my knife in a soft part, and then it must die quickly.

With one hand he explored the body for soft parts. At his touch, it quivered again and tried to kick its bound legs. When he reached the neck, Leo could feel a bag of softer flesh under the wool.

This time, there was no wild wrestling and stabbing. He aimed deliberately. Holding the flesh with one hand, he closed his eyes and made one lunging stab, the sharpest his light frame could muster. With this blow, the blood penetrated the wool so quickly that it ran on to his hand before he withdrew the knife. Not caring now about the sheep escaping, Leo stumbled away, stiff and bruised, still clutching the knife.

Finding dry stuff for a fire got to be as difficult as running the sheep down. He became aware how sore he felt as he bent over to saw off with the knife handfuls of the little dried grass he could find. Only a few tufts of grass growing hard against some of the stones were long or dry enough to burn. All the rest was cropped close and looked green and juicy. Each time he returned to the sacrifice, Leo hoped that all sign of life in the sheep would be gone. It appeared to be still enough to be dead. It didn't disturb the soft grasses packed against it.

Odd sticks of prickly hawthorn and scotch thistle made the pile grow quicker, but Leo managed to collect only enough fuel to build against one side of the sheep, and even then his pyre barely rose as high as the animal's back. When he attempted to light it, he found that the grass wasn't as dry as it looked, and he struck match after match, breaking more than he lit. With each flame, he feverishly pressed the grasses against it to encourage them to flare, but the best he could do was to set the pile smouldering and smoking. And he didn't want too much smoke in case that man saw it and came back to the rim of the crater to investigate, but the more he pressed down on the pile, the thicker the smoke that rose up.

He struck another match and thrust it anxiously under the matted and smouldering grass. It gave a sharp crackle and burst into clean yellow flames, forcing Leo to step away quickly with the suddenness of it. A flurry of air in the bowl fanned the blaze, and the leaping flames hid the sheep from Leo's sight for a moment, but just as quickly they died down.

He waited until the fire was just a glow before stepping closer to examine the sacrifice. The acrid smell that wafted up with the last wisps of smoke made him turn away. He stood, bent over, one hand up to his nose, not moving until the nausea subsided.

He plucked up enough courage to face it again. One blackened patch of wool didn't seem much to show for his fire. There wasn't any real shock in that. But then, it happened. A feeble cry came from the opposite side from where he stood. He was sure of it. And then, to make it worse, the body shuddered. It isn't dead! Leo coughed once as his bile welled up again. If God wanted it, why didn't he show me the way?

Sickened, Leo turned and fled from the sacrifice. He couldn't look back. All he saw was the ground just ahead as he scrambled up the slope, sometimes on all fours. Not until he was on the rim of the hill did he stop his flight. A burst of late afternoon sun streamed through the clouds away to the west, and he strained to pick out any sign of God appearing along its strong light.

But he didn't come this time. And when Leo took a last look back, all signs of his burnt offering to God were hidden, as the angle of the setting sun cast a gloomy shadow into the crater's bowl.

Five

'A serious matter . . . yes, a very serious matter —
are you listening to me, Woodmason?' The Head's
voice crackled through the loudspeakers.

Carl was quicker than Woodoh to pull a straight
face — he had to, since he was much taller than
most of the other kids in the grade and easier for
teachers to pick out in a small assembly like this
one out in the yard. But Mr French always kept his
eye on Woodoh. The fart that Fatty Ludovic
made had gone, but the smell hung around, and
Woodoh had trouble keeping a straight face. He
pressed his lips together and stared as innocently
as he could up to the dais beside the flagpole
where Frenchy always stood.

'I just hope for your sake my lad, that you are
not involved in this matter.'

It was always 'matters' with Mr French. The
'matter' of the lunch orders. The 'matter' of the
lost raincoat. The 'matter' of the behaviour on the
school bus.

He went on with his big announcement, the reason for calling these grades of the school together
before going in for the afternoon session. 'It has
been reported to me by Mr Braithwaite, the care-

taker of the Crater Hill reserve, that some time last Sunday afternoon, a senseless act of cruelty was perpetrated on one of the sheep that regularly graze on the hill . . .'

Mr French paused and looked across the assembled grades. A short, neat man, he enjoyed these occasions, using his 'big' voice and some important 'big' words. The way he said words like 'perpetrate' was enough to hold the attention of the assembly, even those who had no idea or even cared about what the word meant.

'Yes, a senseless act of cruelty it was', he repeated deliberately, satisfied that now he had the full attention of his audience.

'This sheep was stabbed in three or four places, and burnt.' He paused for this news to take effect. The response was as he hoped and expected.

'Yes, you may well go ooh!' he said, almost smiling.

Carl and Woodoh glanced sideways at each other. No other sign was needed for both to know that they were thinking about the same thing. Almost together, they looked along their line for a sign of Peter, but he wasn't within sight. Frenchy must have been looking straight at them.

'Yes Woodmason, I know you find it difficult to be serious about anything. And your mate Carl Forster there beside you. This matter concerns you as much as anyone else in the school, so I would be obliged if you two would give it the attention it deserves.'

'Yes sir', they mumbled together, looking down at the asphalt.

'Now what makes this whole business very nasty

for us, is that Mr Braithwaite is sure that the person responsible was a boy either from the lower forms of the High School, or the upper grades from St Joseph's, or here. He saw a boy of about that size up amongst the sheep on Sunday afternoon. Now, who knows anything about this matter?'

Everyone stood still and silent, sharing a guilt that belonged to only one of them. Woodoh and Carl stared straight ahead, neither willing to be the one to tell about seeing the new kid up there last Saturday. Not yet, anyway.

Across the lines in the other grade, Peter was trying to sneak a look at Leo, but he could see only a part of his face, not enough to work out what he was thinking. Peter wondered what Leo would say to Frenchy. Would he tell him that stuff about God? Perhaps he wouldn't own up to anything. It didn't look as if he was going to say anything here, or he would've put his hand up by now.

Leo's hands stayed in the pockets of his jeans, one hand fingering a handkerchief, the other tightly clenched. Only half-listening to the Head, he was thinking about the cry of the sheep. He had only half-listened to everyone since Sunday when he returned from the hill to face Rick and his angry hands, and his mother's questions and tears. A stinging blow to the ear hadn't shut out the cry of the sheep for long. When his pillow had soaked up the pain, he could still hear the pathetic baa of his sacrifice, and strain as he might, Leo hadn't been able to bring back the vision of God to tell him what to do next.

Those first few days afterwards, his teacher,

Miss Campieri, must have thought he looked sick, because she didn't nag him for not paying attention. She had been kind to Leo right from when he started at Manoora, and he liked her straight away too, if only at first because her hair was even redder than his own, and she had just as many freckles, which Leo had always thought went away when you grew up.

'Well', Mr French went on, 'if no one is going to come forward and speak up now, then we shall have to use other methods to find the culprit if he's here at this school.'

He often threatened like that at one of these assemblies. Leo's numbed feelings, rather than fear alone, kept him riveted to his spot in the line. The voice through the microphone made one last appeal.

'If anyone wishes to tell me anything, they can come to the office after school, is that clear?'

'Yes Mr French', many murmured.

'Right teachers, you may take your classes inside now.'

The tension was broken, and several kids began to fidget as they often did after standing in line for a time.

'Will we say anything?' Carl whispered, head down, as they started to file into school.

Woodoh didn't answer him, but risked a warning nudge. He was sure the Head had his eye on them as they walked closer to the dais. Woodoh's warning made Carl look up too suddenly, and his eyes met the knowing stare of Mr French. Woodoh managed one of his cheeky grins and kept walking. They both expected a voice to bring them

41

back, but they moved on quite unchallenged.

Woodoh waited until they were turning from the corridor to their classroom. 'Phew, that was close!' he blurted out. 'What did you want to go and do that for right under Frenchy's nose, you twit!'

'I didn't know he was staring at us', answered Carl, guiltily, 'but anyway, we haven't done anything...'

He didn't get the chance to say any more. Their class teacher, Mr Reynolds, had long before put them in different groups, so any more talk would have to wait now until afternoon recess. And it seemed to take ages to come.

They didn't have to go looking for Peter. He was waiting for them as they came out into the yard.

'Woodoh, are you two going to tell about seeing Leo Farrell up on Crater?' he asked.

'Let's go down to the grass', was all Woodoh replied, nodding his head in that direction.

They followed him away from the crowded games area and down to the rougher part of the yard where a few stunted trees bordered a stretch of well-worn grass.

Peter waited until they were apart from any other kids before repeating his question. 'Are you going to tell?'

Woodoh wrinkled his nose. 'Why should we?' he said.

'Didn't you hear Frenchy say that the sheep had been stabbed?'

'So what?'

'Well, it's a bit different from chasing them,

42

isn't it?'

'Yeah, but we didn't see him stab the silly sheep, did we?' said Woodoh, as if to convince himself as much as the others.

'It could've been someone else', added Carl.

'Oh come on', said Peter, shaking his head, 'we saw him chasing sheep up there just the day before'.

'But you said he couldn't catch one, didn't you?' said Woodoh.

'Yeah.'

'So you see, it could've been someone else.'

'Nup, it was him, I bet.'

'Where is he now?' asked Carl.

Peter looked up, searching the playing areas. 'I don't think he's come out. Sometimes he stays inside at recess time.'

'What does he do inside?' asked Carl.

'I dunno, just messes around I suppose. He must read or something.'

'I don't reckon we ought to dob him in', said Woodoh. It was more an order than an idea.

'Neither do I', said Carl.

'Why not?'

Woodoh shrugged his shoulders. 'Oh I dunno, he hasn't done anything to us, has he?' he said.

'Nup', Carl agreed, 'and he's a bit of a weaky too, I reckon'.

Peter didn't like the idea of telling on Leo either, but he thought that killing a sheep was even worse than pinching something. 'He did kill a sheep, though', he said.

Woodoh shook his head. 'Frenchy didn't say that.'

'Yes he did.'

'No he didn't. He just said that it was stabbed in three or four places.'

'And he said it was burnt', Carl reminded Woodoh.

'It must have been as good as dead then', said Peter.

Woodoh didn't want to be bothered any more. 'Oh come on, let's forget it', he said, breaking away and heading across the grass towards a group of boys kicking a football.

'Yeah, come on, let's have a kick before we have to go in', said Carl, pulling Peter's arm.

But they weren't allowed to forget it.

Six

'Gary, Mr French would like to see you', was all Mr Reynolds said as he culled Woodoh out from the stream filing into the classes. Carl hung back from going in as though expecting he would be asked to stay behind too, but their teacher smiled and added, 'just Gary this time, Carl; you go inside now'.

Woodoh stood for a moment, hoping Mr Reynolds might tell him what the Head wanted him for, but if he knew, he wasn't telling right now.

'Well go on, what are you waiting for?' he said. And that was all.

Woodoh tried to look his usual cocky self as he stood outside the Head's door waiting for him to answer the knock. A couple of girls going past the hall pointed at him and giggled. He made a silent gesture in return with both face and hand. The office door swung open and he quickly straightened up.

Frenchy looked down at him. 'Ah, Woodmason', he said, smiling, 'come along in will you'.

Woodoh followed him into the office and stood with his hands clasped behind his back while

Frenchy settled himself on the other side of the table. The Head shuffled a few papers, then, with a flourish, he removed his glasses, bent forward on one elbow, and stared intently at him.

'Now laddie, you know something about this matter, don't you?' he said.

'Me, sir?'

Frenchy pointed dramatically at him. 'Yes, my bright young rooster — you!' His animal names were reserved for kids like Woodoh.

Woodoh made one more weak attempt to sound innocent. 'I don't know what you mean, sir', he mumbled.

Frenchy cut him off. 'Oh yes you do. I've known you for some years now, right from the time you were a little tyke in the lower grades, and I can read the signs. You can't hide anything from me, Woodmason — you and that friend of yours, Carl Forster, know something about this sheep business, don't you? I'd be surprised if you actually did the deed, but you know something. Out with it now.'

Woodoh wondered how long he would be able to hold out without saying anything.

'I have plenty of time', said the Head, shuffling his papers around again.

The silence went on and on, broken only by paper shuffling or a scraping foot. Frenchy made the first move.

'Well then, we'll see if Master Forster can tell me anything that you can't', he said.

Woodoh saw at once that he wasn't bluffing as he watched him go to the intercom and ask Mr Reynolds to send Carl to the office. Then back

46

to the paper-shuffling, without any expression.

Woodoh didn't turn round when Carl knocked on the door. And he didn't dare look at him either when Frenchy called him in. He made them stand side by side, facing him across the desk. Frenchy stared straight at Carl.

'Now what have you got to add to this story, Forster?'

Carl tried to feign innocence. 'What story, sir?'

'You know very well what story — this sheep-stabbing business. Your friend here and I have been having a little chat about it.'

Now Woodoh knew that all was lost. Carl would think that he'd told. Sure enough, Frenchy won in the end.

'We only saw the new kid Farrell chasing sheep', said Carl.

'Who's we?' asked Frenchy.

Carl looked puzzled, shrugging his shoulders. 'Me and Woodoh and Peter Birchell', he said.

'Woodoh, as you call him, Peter, and I', corrected the Head.

'Yes sir, that's what I said.'

'Well, Woodmason?' said Frenchy turning, and smiling in triumph.

Woodoh gave up without further struggle. 'Yes sir, we saw him chasing a sheep on Saturday. But we weren't up at the reserve on Sunday. That's all we know.'

'Then why has it taken so long to get it out of you, eh?' said Frenchy, tapping the desk with his finger.

'I dunno.'

'Well I know why, it's because of some silly idea

that says you don't "dob in" your mates, isn't it?'

Woodoh murmured, 'Yes sir'.

The Head leaned back in his chair as though he was finished with them. Woodoh shuffled, waiting for the next move.

'You two can wait over there; I haven't finished with you yet', said Frenchy, pointing to a spot just inside the door.

Next came Peter. He didn't even try to stall, so it didn't take Frenchy long to get out of him his side of the story, and then he too was stood over against the office wall beside the other two.

And then Leo. If he noticed the other three boys standing there, he gave no sign as he walked right up to the edge of the desk in response to the Head's call soon after he had appeared outside the office.

All that Woodoh and his mates could see of Leo was his back and the fingers of his hands clasping and unclasping. They could see Frenchy's face frowning and his bushy eyebrows crinkling up over his glasses.

'Well my lad, I don't know you very well, do I?'

Woodoh thought that was a funny way to start putting the kid on the mat. Leo didn't look up. He shook his bowed head only once.

'Haven't you got a tongue?'

Leo's reply was mumbled down his front.

'Speak up lad, I'm not going to hurt you.'

The others heard a louder, 'Yes sir'.

'Now, did you hear everything I said out at that assembly this afternoon?'

'Yes sir.'

'And you know something about that sheep,

don't you?'

No answer. Leo was thinking of words to explain about God.

The Head leaned forward, resting his folded arms on the desk. 'Don't you try wasting my time too, laddie. You might as well tell me about it now. I'll get to the truth in the end, you know. Ask Woodmason over there, he'll tell you, won't you Woodmason?'

What could Woodoh say except, 'Yes sir'.

Leo didn't turn to look at the others. He was still thinking of answers, still uncertain. His mouth remained tightly closed, twitching at the corners as he thought.

The Head kept up the pressure. 'You see, I know you were chasing sheep up on Crater Hill last Saturday', he said, wagging a forefinger, 'so let's start there shall we? What were you doing that for?'

It couldn't be put off any longer. The Head was about to repeat the question, when Leo suddenly looked up and spoke as if he were reciting the words. 'I caught it for God.'

Woodoh and the others watched the surprised reaction on Frenchy's face. And then a kind of boiling up.

'Now look here young fella, don't play games with me. What sort of an excuse is that? What have Mr Braithwaite's sheep got to do with God may I ask?'

He didn't give Leo any chance to answer. 'No, it won't do, Farrell', he went on, 'you'll have to dream up a better story than that, and you'd better be quick about it'.

Peter took a step forward. 'Please sir', he interrupted, 'that's what he told us he was trying to catch the sheep for'.

The Head looked disbelievingly at Peter. 'Do you mean to tell me that he told you the same story — that he was running after sheep for God?'

'Yes sir, he did.'

The Head turned to Leo. 'And was it by any chance for God that you stabbed and burnt one of those poor animals up on the hill?'

Without hesitation, Leo nodded. That really sent Frenchy off. He wasn't the sort to strap or hit anyone, but he could get mad with his voice when he wanted to.

'I've heard some rare excuses in my time, but I didn't ever think any boy would try to tell me that he committed an act of cruelty like this for God', he said, his voice rising and his face growing redder. 'You'd better explain yourself, boy!'

But he gained little satisfaction from Leo, who stood woodenly before him, either nodding or shaking his head, any words of explanation gone now before the onslaught of fiery questions. The nearest to any answer came when Leo murmured, 'Abraham did it'.

The Head calmed himself down and tried another tack. He appealed to the others to help him with Leo. Woodoh and Carl shrugged. It was beyond them. While Peter had first thought they should tell on Leo, now he was feeling sorry for him standing trapped in front of Frenchy's desk.

'I think he means Abraham from the Bible', he said, trying to be helpful.

'That doesn't tell me anything I don't know already, Birchell', said the Head testily, and with that he sent them back to their classrooms, but he kept Leo.

'To let you stew over your story a bit more', he told him.

Leo was still there 'stewing' at the end of the afternoon when everyone else was about to go home. The Head had tried everything — more shouting, coaxing, and badgering, but mostly he left him alone in silence while he went on with other work. He believed that making boys stand for a long time without saying anything to them was usually the best way to get the truth out of them. When they were finally permitted to speak, they often owned up to everything.

But this boy was different, he had to admit that. Just that tom-fool yarn about killing the sheep for God, that was all he had got out of him after an hour or more. He would have to let him go soon.

Though he didn't think much of the way young Miss Campieri ran her class, it was just possible that she might help to extract the true story from the boy, so, as a last resort, he called her to the office. He made the most of this final speech, directing it at Leo's teacher, but really still speaking to the boy who stood at one end of the desk so that each could see the other two faces.

'Well Miss Campieri, I suppose you've been wondering why this lad has been up here with me in the office for so long?' He went on before she could reply. 'He is the perpetrator of the deed of which I spoke at the lunchtime assembly. Yes, he took a knife to one of Mr Braithwaite's sheep. He has admitted it.'

Anna Campieri looked hard at Leo. His eyes returned her gaze steadily enough, but they looked blankly beyond her, expressing neither guilt nor shame. She wanted to say something to him, but this wasn't the moment.

The Head talked on. 'But what is perhaps the worst feature of this whole dreadful business is the excuse he trots out. He tells me, and some of the other boys, that he killed the sheep for God! Now I ask you Miss Campieri, have you ever heard anything more ridiculous in your life? I know I haven't. In all my years of dealing with boys and their mischief, and girls as well, I have never heard anything to equal it, and believe me, boys have tried me out with some funny excuses for their misdemeanours. Can you imagine, Miss Campieri, any boy having the nerve to blame an act like this on God?

'Now, unfortunately, he refuses to tell me the real reason for this wilful act of murder — yes murder, for that is how I regard it. Farrell, have you anything to tell your class teacher here that you haven't told me, because I am sure she will be glad to hear it, won't you Miss Campieri?'

Anna could feel the challenge in the question, not just to Leo standing there, mute before the flurry of words, but to herself, and to her way of handling her class. She chose her words carefully.

'Yes, I would like to hear anything Leo has to say about it. Could I perhaps have a quiet word alone with him for a moment please, Mr French?' she asked.

The Head snorted. 'If you think you can get any more out of him that way, then go ahead. Take him, he's all yours.'

Anna chose a bench in the school garden at the front of the school, not a spot where other children would pass on their way out. She motioned Leo to sit beside her. He did as she asked, but stared straight ahead. She half-turned to face him.

'Leo, what did God look like?' she asked quietly.

The question made it easier for him to turn and look at her. She was the first to understand. He could tell her and she wouldn't laugh or shout at him.

'You can tell me Leo', she said.

And he knew she meant it. He looked away again, searching the garden for nothing more than its friendly patterns. The pursed mouth relaxed and the words came out as he thought of them, no longer locked in.

'You can see through him', he said.

'Was he old or young?' asked Anna.

'He wasn't much like a person.'

'Oh?'

'He had too many points.'

'Points?'

'They were all glittery.'

'Like a star?'

'A bit like, but more colours — the cloak had all sorts of colours in it.'

'Cloak?'

'Yes, he was nearly all wrapped up in it with lots of folds and creases. It flashed as he moved.'

'Did he speak?'

'Sort of.'

53

'Like us?'

'Oh no, it was long and slow, and it kept going.'

'Like an echo?'

'I suppose.'

'Did he call your name?'

'Yes.'

'Did it sound like this — Lee-ee-ee-ee-oh-oh-oh-ohhh?' She made her voice trail softly away.

'Yes, something like that.'

'Are you sure it wasn't wind or . . .' She couldn't think of anything else.

'No', he said emphatically.

She sensed his hurt at her doubting, but she pressed on with her questions. 'And about the sheep, Leo — did God ask you to kill it for him?'

Mention of the sheep made him look away from her. She thought he might refuse to answer any more questions, but after staring at the ground for a moment, he faced her again.

'God sort of pointed to it', he said haltingly, 'and . . . and then I knew what he meant, because . . . because in the Bible, they always made a sacrifice like that'.

'Are you sure?'

'Yes', he nodded, 'I know the story about Abraham and the sheep that was caught by the horns, the one he gave to God in place of his son Isaac'.

'Oh, I see, that's the one.'

Anna was beginning to feel lost. 'Are you quite sure that God wanted you to offer a sheep just like it was in that old, old Bible story?' she asked.

Leo nodded again. Anna sat in silence, trying to think of a right way out. The boy was not lying, she was positive of that, but how would anyone like Mr French understand him when she felt so helpless herself.

With a sigh, she stood up. Looking down on the boy still sitting stiffly on the bench, she wanted to crouch down and give him a reassuring hug, but she doubted if Mr French would understand that. Leo mightn't want it himself, anyway. There was nothing more she could do right now, but she stood, putting off the moment of return to the Head, rehearsing in her mind a sympathetic version of Leo's story. She gave that up and made her decision — truth would serve Leo's cause best.

'Come Leo', she said, touching his arm, 'we must go inside and see Mr French again before you go home'.

Leo's face walled off again, but his rigid body responded to her touch, and he obediently stood up and followed her.

Seven

'Why us?' moaned Woodoh.

'Because we were unlucky enough to see this nit chasing a sheep, that's why', said Carl, glaring back at Leo walking beside Peter, a pace or two behind them.

'Frenchy wants to pay us back for not owning up straight away', said Peter.

'Yeah', agreed Carl, 'he knows old Braithwaite is always on to us about anything that happens in the reserve. You'd better own up straight away, Farrell, or we'll cop it too.'

Leo nodded.

'Yeah, well just remember that when we get there', added Carl.

First thing the following day, the Head had sent them off to face Braithwaite. It was the only punishment he could think of.

He had agreed with Miss Campieri on one point — that strange boy Farrell probably was telling the truth, but he had to punish him somehow. He was rather glad to pass the boy over to someone else. After all, the damned affair didn't have all that much to do with the school — the killing had been carried out at the weekend, not on a school-day, and it wasn't as if the boy had been a pupil at the school for very long. It wasn't the same as having a Manoora-born boy behaving like that.

He had unearthed the culprit, so let Braithwaite himself decide what to do with the fellow. He'd be sure to give him a scare, and that could be the end of it.

'What if he's not there?' asked Peter, as they came within sight of Braithwaite's.

'So we go back to school again', said Woodoh.

'Frenchy won't like that.'

'So what? Let's find out first.' Woodoh looked over into the front yard as though to check if the coast was clear before opening the gate.

Peter walked further on to the end of the hedge and took a quick look up to Crater Hill. 'He's not out on this side of the reserve', he called.

'He's not in the front yard, either', said Woodoh. 'Come on, let's go in.'

They entered and filed across the yard, skirting around a couple of old-model cars parked on the worn grass. None of the boys seemed keen to be the one to knock, and they bunched together on the front verandah, with Leo standing a few paces apart. After some whispering and nudging amongst the three, Woodoh opened the fly-wire door and gave the front door a timid knock. He quickly closed the wire door and stood well away from it. Nobody answered the knock.

More urging made him try a louder knock. His hand was barely raised when a voice rasped out from behind them. 'What d'you kids want?'

Taken by surprise, they all jumped and turned around. It was a relief for Woodoh and Carl to find it wasn't old Braithwaite. They recognized the caretaker's son, pretty big like his father, and nearly as tough-looking.

'We have to see Mr Braithwaite', said Woodoh.

'He's not here — I think he's on the tractor up in the reserve somewhere. Just a minute.'

He sprang on to the verandah, opened the front door and poked his head inside. 'Mum!' his voice rang through the house.

'What?'

'Some kids here to see the old man!'

'Right!'

He turned and looked down at the four boys. 'Watcha want him for?'

'It's about his sheep', said Peter.

The son made a face. 'Huh, if it's about that dead one, I hope none of you kids had anything to do with it. The old man's hopping mad about it.'

And with that good news, he gave Leo's hair a friendly ruffle, jumped down from the verandah and walked over to one of the cars. Woodoh and Carl watched, mesmerized, as the engine roared into life and the car backed and swerved across the grass, then out through the driveway.

Peter looked at Leo who was standing, staring at nothing. 'Aren't you scared?' he asked.

'Yes', said Leo, without showing any sign of it.

'You don't look it.'

'He will', said Carl grimly.

'What d'you think he'll do to us?' asked Peter.

'It'll be O.K. if we get a chance to tell him why we're here before he goes mad', said Woodoh.

'I vote you do the talking, Woodoh', said Carl.

'So do I', said Peter.

'Well boys, what can I do for you?' It was Mrs Braithwaite cutting in on their talk. She looked big too, standing there arms folded, propping open the wire screen door, but her smile and deep voice sounded friendly enough.

'Mr French sent us to see Mr Braithwaite', said Woodoh.

'Oh yes, and what's it all about then?'

Woodoh looked around at the others, unsure whether to tell her. He didn't get any help from them.

'Well we . . . we . . .', he started, 'we . . . had to bring this kid to tell him something'.

'He's not here right now, do you want to wait?'

Woodoh looked at the others again and shrugged his shoulders. They shrugged back.

'Ask her for how long', whispered Carl.

'Probably about half an hour before he drops back by the house', said Mrs Braithwaite, who had clearly heard the whispering.

'We'd better wait then', said Woodoh, not anxious to return to Frenchy without a fair excuse.

'Suit yourselves, but see you stay on the verandah. If it's what I think you've come about, then you'd better sit right where you are and not wander about.'

Without any more prompting, the three quickly sat down in a line along the edge of the verandah. And then Leo, too. Smiling a little at their quick reaction, Mrs Braithwaite closed the door and disappeared inside.

They didn't say much to each other as they waited. They mostly stared at the ground at their feet, kicking idly at the dirt or picking up an odd stone within their reach and dropping it again, anything to cover their nervousness. Leo sat quite still, not glancing sideways as the others were doing now and then. His body remained tensed, his freckled hands gripped his knees firmly.

It began to look as though they might get out of facing Braithwaite that day, when the tell-tale sound of a tractor approaching made them all look up together and watch the gateway for his arrival. It wasn't long before the tractor swung into the yard and bounced to a halt just across the grass from where they sat. Braithwaite slowly removed his ear mufflers and climbed down from the seat, all the while eyeing the boys with a knowing look.

'Well, well, if it isn't my friends Woodmason and Forster. So now you've taken to knocking off my sheep have you?'

'No', protested Woodoh.

'What d'you mean, no? Don't give me that. I know why you lot are squatting on my verandah.'

Woodoh didn't like it, but he couldn't put off telling. 'Mr French made us bring over this kid Farrell', he said. 'We saw him last Saturday chasing your sheep up on Crater Hill.'

Braithwaite came up close to Woodoh and gripped him under the chin with one hand, forcing him to look up straight into his eyes. 'So you're trying to tell me that you and your mates have come over just to bring this squirt here. That's a likely yarn. I can check up on you, you know.'

'It's true', said Carl, who could see that Woodoh's mouth was locked up under old

Braithwaite's strong grip.

Braithwaite let him go, swung round, and poked at Peter with his thick grubby finger. 'What about you? Where do you fit in?'

'He was the one who first saw the kid chasing sheep', said Carl, 'he was with us up the cypress trees'.

'So, you were climbing those trees again. I might have guessed you two couldn't be up in the reserve without breaking rules. Is that true, is this the kid who carved up one of my sheep?' Braithwaite demanded of Peter.

'Have you lost your tongue?' he shouted, when Peter didn't answer straight away.

Peter shook his head.

'Were you in it too? Come on, out with it!'

Leo spoke up. 'I did it on my own', he said, quietly.

'Oh really, did you? That's pretty hard to swallow', said Braithwaite sarcastically as he sized him up, 'though I must say I had a feeling the kid I saw chasing my sheep had red hair, and you're the only one of this little mob with it. How did you manage it on your own then? What did you use, eh?'

'A knife.'

'What sort of knife?'

'A kitchen knife.'

'Then tell me this — why the hell did you use it on one of my sheep?'

Leo didn't want to give the God reason any more, but Braithwaite shook it out of him. At first, he thought Leo was trying to be funny, and that made him angrier than ever. He spat on the ground, grabbed Leo, and pulled him close. Leo didn't blink or try to turn away.

'Listen kid, I wasn't born yesterday. You haven't heard from any bloody spirit up there', Braithwaite said, pointing skywards, 'so let's have the real reason, and quick!'

'Well?' he growled, as Leo opened his mouth to take a breath before answering.

'I saw God up there on the hill', said Leo as evenly as he could, held as he was by the shirt-front, 'and he asked me to do it'.

Braithwaite flung him off with disgust. 'He's nuts!' he said to the others, who stood in an un-happy row, 'but nuts or not, I'm going to make him finish the job. Get round the back, and I'll show you something. You others come and look too!'

He gave Leo a prod, making him stumble for-ward. More prodding steered him around the house and into another yard behind it. There was even less garden there than at the front. Here it was old tractor parts strewn about on the ground between iron sheds, scattered drums, some on end, some on their side, and one greasy old sheep tethered to a piece of machinery, with only worn grass within range. Braithwaite gave the sheep a slap on the flank as he went past.

'Why didn't you carve up mangy old Ruth here?' he sneered, 'she's just a useless pet of the wife's — only good for pet food, too. But let's look at a real mess.'

He ushered them further down the yard. Woodoh and the others watched as Leo was forced to look behind a screening fence, and they saw him turn away, very white and sick-looking.

'What d'you think of your work now?' said Braithwaite, holding him as though he expected him to turn tail and run. 'Come on you others, come and see the damage.'

They edged up to the fence until they could just see round it. The rubbish-heap was ready for burning, and atop of it, the body of the half-burnt sheep that Braithwaite had brought down from Crater Hill had been flung. As it was not summer, the bloodied and partly blackened animal wasn't alive with flies, but ants by the million crawled all over it, and the stench was rising strong.

'Go on, look at it!' insisted Braithwaite, gripping the back of Leo's neck, 'and when you've had enough, I'm going to get you to finish the job you started. Your God won't mind, will he?'

After Braithwaite released him, Leo stood with his head hanging down, trying to avoid facing the rubbish heap and its stinking carcase. When Braithwaite left them and disappeared into a shed, the other three moved away to the other side of the fence. They whispered amongst themselves.

'Farrell must be crazy staying there by that stinking heap', said Carl.

'He's probably not game to move', said Woodoh.

'I don't blame him — Braithwaite will be back in a minute', said Peter, indicating the shed.

Braithwaite did emerge soon after, carrying a drum and some old rags. He threw the rags on the ground and doused them with an oily black fluid from the can.

'Pick up the rags and stuff them under the sheep', he ordered.

Leo automatically did as he was told. The others moved forward and watched, more comfortable now that the smell of oil was helping to suppress the stench. When Leo had finished, Braithwaite stepped up and emptied all the remaining oil from the drum over the dead body.

'Right, here you are', he said, tossing a box of matches near to Leo, 'finish the job'.

Distaste now for any reminder of the sacrifice and fear of the likely flare-up combined to hamper Leo's attempts to light the pile. He threw each lighted match from too far away and they blew out. After three vain attempts, Braithwaite angrily snatched the box of matches from him, struck one match and tossed it deftly on to the rags.

Mrs Braithwaite was standing just inside the back door of the house, trying to make out what was going on down the yard. She saw the sudden gush of flame, and then dark plumes of smoke rising from the rubbish heap, and guessed. She saw three of the boys step back suddenly from the heat. She saw her husband standing right behind the red-headed boy to prevent him backing away. And she saw the boy trying to shield his eyes from the blast of the heat and his nose from the smell. She turned away herself, then.

Afterwards, she waited at the front door until she saw the boys leaving. She called them back, and offered them each a biscuit from a tin. Woodoh and Carl and Peter took one, but Leo shook his head. Eyeing the signs of his queasiness,

Mrs Braithwaite didn't press him to take one. On the way back to school, Woodoh and Carl munched theirs cheerfully enough. Peter threw his away.

He found he had no stomach for it.

Eight

Anna Campieri hesitated at the door of the shop. She wasn't looking forward to meeting Leo's parents like this. She wished that Mr French had invited them to the school instead of asking her to deliver a note to them. She'd never been asked to make a home visit of this kind before — all her other meetings with parents had been at school.

She would try to see the mother first. She braced herself, gripped the doorknob, and opened the door. The shop was empty apart from a man behind the counter. He got up from a stool, hastily wiping crumbs from his mouth as he swallowed the remains of a bread roll. A few crumbs hung around his front.

'Good evening, what can I get you?' he said, swallowing.

If this was Leo's father, there wasn't any likeness.

'Is Mrs Farrell in?' Anna asked.

'Eh?' he replied, a bit confused at finding she knew Nola's name.

'She does live here, doesn't she?'

He nodded, 'Are you a saleswoman or something? You're a bit late in the day, aren't you?'

'No, I'm not. I just want to see Mrs Farrell for a moment.'

'Oh', he said, pausing to give her time to tell him more.

She didn't.

He looked hard at her, then went to the door behind the shop. 'Nola!' he called, 'shop!'

He came back, leant on the counter, and eyed her again. 'I haven't seen you in the shop before', he said.

'No, I live more at the other end of the town.'

'Oh. How did you get to know Nola? We haven't been in Manoora much more than a month.'

'I don't know her. I'm Leo's teacher at school.'

He straightened up. 'Oh are you? What's he been up to?'

Anna didn't want to say anything yet, before seeing the mother. 'Are you Mr Farrell?' she asked.

'Me? No I'm not Leo's father, thank God. He popped off five or six years ago. Not much of a loss for Nola, really. He was pretty hopeless apparently. We've been running a couple of other shops together since. The name's Rick Nugent, what's yours?'

'Campieri, Anna Campieri.'

'Brought up in this town?'

'No, I've only been here two and a half years.'

He grinned. 'Thought you didn't look like a local.'

Anna risked one question of him. 'Mr Nugent, is Mrs Farrell a religious person?'

The friendly expression faded. 'What's that got to do with it?'

'Oh, just that Leo seems to know quite a lot about the Bible for a boy of his age.'

At that moment, Leo's mother came through to the shop, wiping her hands down the sides of a smock, then pushing back a wisp of hair. Rick glanced at her, but spoke to Anna.

'Yeah, well that's because his mother here pumped all that mumbo-jumbo into him when he was little. Not as much now though.'

Nola looked from one to the other, confused.

'This is Leo's teacher', said Rick, 'she was asking whether you were religious, because that son of yours must have been spouting the Bible at school. All I can say is good luck to her for getting that much out of him — it's more than I can.'

He laughed. 'Perhaps he knows it's all wasted on me. But I'll bet he's lazy at everything else at school if he's running true to form. He's never around when there's work to be done, that's for sure.'

A customer came in and saved Anna from any more. Rick gestured to Nola to take the visitor through to the back of the shop. They moved down the passage and into a sitting-room. The television flickered on with the sound turned down. Anna accepted the invitation to sit and chose a chair facing away from the screen. Sitting opposite her, with light from the television on her face, Leo's mother looked white and tired, dark shadows masking the real blue of her eyes.

'What about Leo?' she asked.

Anna glanced across to an open door leading to another room. 'Is he around at the moment?' she asked.

Nola shook her head. 'I think he'll be upstairs in his room, probably doing something with his dioramas. He spends all his spare time with them.'

'Dioramas?' Anna looked puzzled.

'Yes, they are scenes he makes and sets up inside scrap boxes from the shop. He's always playing with them or making a new one', answered Nola, pausing between each sentence. 'He keeps them stacked in his wardrobe and cupboards. He brought them with him to the two shops we've been in since . . . He's never thrown any of them away or left them behind when we've shifted.'

'What are the scenes about?' asked Anna.

Nola shook her head and shrugged. 'Oh, I only get to peep inside them now and then if he leaves one out. He wouldn't want anyone fiddling with them, but of the two or three I've seen, one was like Noah's Ark and the other looked a bit like the inside of a volcano, and, oh yes, he did show both of us a nativity scene he made last Christmas. A funny boy, Leo.'

'Is he very interested in religion, Mrs Farrell?'

'I've always taken him to church with me, yes.'

'I gather Mr Nugent doesn't go?'

'No. Rick isn't like me, but he does work hard in the shop, he's good like that. But what is it about Leo?'

It couldn't be put off any longer. Anna took the note from her bag and handed it over. Frowning, Leo's mother turned the envelope over a couple of times.

'It's from the Headmaster, Mr French', said Anna.

'Shall I read it now?'

'Yes, if you want to.'

'Do you know what it's about?'

Anna hesitated. 'I think so, yes.'

Leo's mother looked puzzled. 'Couldn't you just tell me?'

'I think the Head wants you to read his letter, but if you want to ask me about anything in it, then please do. I think that's why he asked me to bring it to you in person.'

Anna had to sit and watch the envelope being slowly opened, the letter unfolded, then read and re-read. She had to watch while Leo's mother put one hand up, squeezing the bridge of her nose as if to hold back tears. But when she looked up from the letter and across to Anna, her eyes were brimming.

'Not Leo, he couldn't have', she said softly, holding out the letter.

Anna took it and read quickly.

Dear Mrs Farrell,

I have the unfortunate duty to inform you that your son Leo has carried out a horrifying atrocity, the like of which I have never experienced in my many years of dealing with youngsters. Leo freely admits to slaughtering a sheep and attempting to burn the carcase. This sheep was the property of a Mr Braithwaite, the caretaker and manager of the Crater Hill Reserve, and whilst your son has had some punishment in the form of facing Mr Braithwaite, I suggest you punish him in your own way and recompense the owner of the sheep for his loss.

Quite apart from the seriousness of this matter, your son put forward as his excuse that he wished to kill the sheep as a sacrifice to God. His teacher, the bearer of this note, believes him, but true or not, his actions suggest that you would be well advised to seek medical advice regarding his mental condition.

I have managed to keep this incident out of the hands of the local police, and I am not taking the extreme step of asking you to withdraw your son from the school, mainly because the size of a town like Manoora would not make it easy for you to place him elsewhere. I shall be watching him closely from now on, and if you wish, you may care to discuss this matter and his progress with me at any convenient time during school hours.

Yours sincerely,

Michael J. French
HEADMASTER

How much worse it sounded, written down like that. Anna tried to think of something to say that might comfort Leo's mother.

'I'm sure you don't need to see about Leo — not yet', she said.

'See who and why?' It was Rick, standing at the door.

Leo's mother didn't answer him.

'All this blubbering, what's brought that on?' he asked, coming over to her. He spotted the letter on the low table between the two women.

'Is this what it's all about?' he asked, picking it up and unfolding it. He didn't wait for her to answer, but started reading it himself. At certain parts, he repeated three or four times in disbelief what the Head had said.

'Your son carrying out a — carrying out a what? . . . Slaughtering a sheep — slaughtering a sheep! . . . Burning the carcase — burning the carcase! . . . A sacrifice to what? A sacrifice to God! . . . Out of the hands of the police! . . . Not asking you to withdraw your son from school — withdraw your son!'

He flung the letter down on the table in front of Leo's mother, then strode around the room waving his arms in anger as he spoke.

'That's just great I don't think, just great! We might as well pack up right now and leave. What hope is there now of building up this heap of a business with this story spreading all around the town. Nobody's going to come to a shop run by the mother of a nut-case who goes around killing the local sheep!'

'Just one sheep, Mr Nugent', Anna reminded him.

'So what?' he said, turning on her and wagging his finger in the air. 'That kid up there might be planning some other mad effort, who knows what he might get up to next.'

He moved close to Leo's mother and bent right over her. 'He's weird that son of yours, can't you face up to that? They'll put him away. This Head-master, French, or whatever his name is, has put his finger right on it, hasn't he — get some medical advice. Haven't I been telling you that? Every chance the kid gets, he sits on his own, poking about with those bloody peep-shows of his. What sort of a boy's game is that? And now — now what new game have we got? Killing a sheep for God!

72

'And that's where you made your big mistake, isn't it — you still think that religion fixes everything. You fed him that stuff, that's all you've done for him. I get more out of him than you do. He works for me when I can catch up with him, and that's because I tell him what to do and see that he does it, that's what he needs.'

'He's working quite well for me at school, Mr Nugent', Anna said, trying to stem the flood.

'So what? He might have a few brains, but they're all scrambled up, and his mother here hasn't helped.'

Anna didn't like to leave Mrs Farrell the way she was, but what could she do to help her with this man present?

'I must be going now, Mrs Farrell', she said, ignoring Rick, 'but please get in touch with me at the school if there's anything else about Leo you would like to discuss. I'll help him to settle in, you can be sure of that.'

'Settle in!' scoffed Rick. 'He won't be causing trouble in this town much longer, I can tell you that.'

'I'm sure people here won't hold it against you, Mr Nugent', said Anna, 'many of them won't even hear about it, and soon it will be forgotten'.

'How would you know, you're not a local, you said so yourself', he said, without respect. 'I know these small places only too well. It'll get around; there'll be no forgetting it.'

'Thank you', said Leo's mother to her, gripping her hand tightly.

For what, Anna thought as she said goodbye to her and left her sitting there fingering the note from the Head again. Following Rick along the passage, Anna was aware of footsteps pattering on the staircase above. She glanced up through the railings but saw no one. She guessed it must have been Leo, who had probably come down closer to listen and then hurried back up when he heard them leave the room.

Poor Leo, he would hear about it soon enough, she thought, and nothing could save him from that.

Nine

As he was fixing a cut-out sheep to a papier-mache Crater Hill, Leo had heard his teacher's voice downstairs. Then the sound of his mother sobbing. No clear words had come up to him before Rick shouted out.

Tip-toeing to the landing, Leo heard enough to know that Miss Campieri must have told them everything. Why would she do that? The boy Woodmason and his mates couldn't help it — they had to tell, but she didn't have to come to the shop.

She had gone now, and it wouldn't be long before one of them came up. And then there would be more shouting and crying.

He heard Rick's heavier footsteps first. Leo left his diorama and sat on the edge of the bed, prepared for trouble.

'Just leave this to me', he heard Rick say from outside the room. So his mother must have come up too.

'I said leave it to me, will you!'

Rick was first into the room. 'Well, what have you got to say for yourself?' he demanded.

Leo couldn't look at him. Rick stepped forward and caught him by a tuft of hair. 'Look at me when I'm speaking to you', he said.

Quickly his mother came and sat beside Leo on the bed, putting an arm around his shoulders. It was meant as a protection, but it hemmed him in even more.

'We're not going to get anywhere, Nola, if you cuddle him like a baby', said Rick, releasing him in disgust.

'Don't shout at him, Rick', said his mother.

'All right, we'll do it your way, we'll take it nice and gentle.' He crouched down to be more on a level with Leo. 'We know what you did to that sheep. And did you know that we will have to pay for it?' he said. 'Did you think of that?'

Leo shook his head.

'Perhaps you might tell us the story about this God of yours — even your mother hasn't ever seen him, have you Nola?'

'Please Rick', she pleaded.

'No, you're the only one who's seen him', he went on, 'doesn't that make you feel extra special? Just think, boy, if I knew how to meet this God you've made up, do you know the first thing I'd ask him to do, do you know, eh?'

'No', answered Leo quietly.

'I'd ask him to wave a magic wand over you so that no more silly ideas came into your head, that's what I'd ask him to do first.'

'Rick, please', his mother interposed again, 'you won't get anywhere with Leo talking like that.'

Unflinchingly, Leo looked straight up at Rick.

'I did see him', he said, emphatically.

This was too much for Rick. He laughed out-right at both of them. 'Oh, I'm sure you did. I'm sure he did, Nola', he scoffed, 'and I suppose this God just floated down out of the sky with all his flapping angels around him, or perhaps he was an up-to-date kind of God and landed in his flying saucer. Is that what happened?'

'No.'

'No, of course it didn't, and I'll tell you why — because you didn't hear from any God, did you? You made it all up as an excuse for going berserk with a knife, didn't you?'

'It wasn't like that', he said, shaking his head.

'Well how was it then, come on, how was it?' Rick taunted.

'I saw him, and I heard him, and he pointed to the sheep.' Leo's voice choked with frustration.

'And that's all — just "I saw him, I heard him, and he pointed to the sheep". You're going to stick to that simple story, are you?' said Rick. 'Then there's nothing you can do with him, Nola. You'd better get him examined and quick, before he takes it into his silly head to do some more damage for his precious God.'

He picked up the diorama from the table beside the bed. 'And while they're examining him, remember to tell them about these bloody things.'

He looked inside it, then swung back to Leo and his mother, and dumped the box on her lap. 'Have a look inside there, and you'll see where he thinks up his weird ideas like this sheep nonsense.'

'What's the harm in these?' she asked, making

an attempt to replace some of the cut-out sheep that had fallen in a heap and slid into the corner of the box.

'It's bloody sick, that's what it is. The only part missing from that little scene is his God.'

He came to Leo and leaned over, close. 'I suppose you can't make a paper God, is that it? Or is it that you don't know what one looks like because you haven't seen one! Which is it, eh?'

Leo didn't look up this time. He wasn't going to say any more to Rick now. What was the use? He wouldn't believe anything, not anything.

'Let me talk to him on my own, Rick', said his mother.

'And what are you going to get out of him with sweet talk and cuddling? What he needs is a bit more of the same I gave him when he came home last Sunday. If I'd only known then what he'd been up to, I'd have . . .'

'He's my boy, Rick', she said.

'And you're welcome to him', said Rick, taking the diorama from her, 'no kid of mine would be fiddling around with these boxes of junk.'

He tore at the sides of the box, opening them out flat to expose the scene built up on the base. He tried crushing the papier-mache hill with the palm of his hand, but when it stood up to this treatment, he dropped the whole diorama to the floor. Some of the model sheep fell away from it, but the ones that stayed glued in place were ground under his foot along with the hill and the rest of the scene. It happened too quickly for Leo's mother to try to stop him, but when he moved to the cupboard where Leo's other dioramas were stored, she got up from the bed and tried to prevent him taking them out.

'Don't Rick, don't', she cried, 'don't touch the others'.

'You're too soft', he said, easily pushing her aside, 'that's been the trouble all along'.

'Leave him to me', she tried once more.

'Look, this is the first thing that has to be done to get those crackbrain ideas out of his head.'

He turned and wrenched open the door of the cupboard. One after the other he pulled out the dioramas. He gave them all the same treatment. The boxes, the coloured cellophanes, the figures and the scenery from each tableau were crumpled and crushed before joining the others in a heap in the corner.

Leo's mother tried to restrain him, but she pulled and shouted in vain. She offered little more resistance than one of the paper figures, and Rick's shouting drowned her's. Finally she cried that this would be the end between them, and he yelled back that it was all the same to him, he'd had enough of her and her son and the rotten businesses they'd tried to run together with him doing most of the hard work.

Leo put his hands to his ears, but, as if mesmerized, he watched the demolition of his precious scenes. Most of the small figures he had spent so long in fashioning were now hidden beneath the crumpled mess of the outer shells. Why did Rick hate him as much as this? Was it because he knew that Leo hated him sometimes, but not always, not enough to make Rick do this, to destroy his dioramas? They were questions posed more through blind disbelief than through anger. Swallowing didn't shift the dry lump in his throat, and no tears welled up to help his feelings break out. His was a silent frustration of helplessness.

The corner of the room became an untidy graveyard for all Leo's figures and scenes. With the last one of them despatched, Rick kicked the boxes into a pile. 'Now clean up the bloody mess and forget them, do you hear me!' he said, then stamped out, slamming the door.

Leo hardly responded when his mother moved to comfort him. He sat woodenly under her arm, not burying his head into her shoulder as she hoped. She left him, went to the pile, knelt down and began foraging through it, hoping to salvage something from the wreck for him. One horse and rider she uncovered appeared unscathed.

'Look Leo . . .', she began, holding it up.

But before she could say more, he was up from the bed and at the door, pulling at the handle.

'Leo, wait!' she called, getting up from the floor.

There was no stopping him. Down the stairs and into the darkened closed shop.

'Leo, wait!' she cried out from the landing.

Rick heard the clatter of footsteps, and came out from the living-room. When he reached the shop, the street door was unlatched and ajar. He didn't make any attempt to chase Leo or even look out into the street before he shut and bolted the door.

'Serves him right if he can't get back till morning', he muttered, and went back through the shop and the house to secure the back door as well.

Ten

It wasn't a night to be out. A cold, sneaky wind
flung drops of rain at Leo's face. Crater Hill drew
him again irresistibly, and he ran in that direction
for as long as street lights lit the way. He slowed to
a walk under the last of the lights. It threw a weak
beam down on to the entrance to the reserve
where a white gate barred the roadway. Though
closed each night to keep out cars, it couldn't stop
anyone walking up to Crater Hill. An old turn-
stile, free of any bars or locks, stood near the gate.
Leo had to push hard on it, but after an alarm-
ingly long and loud squeak, it turned its quarter-
circle to let him pass into the reserve.

To him, the fence seemed to be the boundary
between light and dark. Now, the street lamp
didn't help at all to penetrate the velvety void
that lay ahead of him, giving no hint of grass,
of cypress trees, or rising ground. It was scramble
and fall, scramble and fall from now on. Even
after his eyes grew used to the dark, he still
blundered forward. Cypress branches loomed up
and whipped him before he could stop and
change direction. His hands grew cold and numb
as he flung them out to ward off branches, to

break his falls when he stumbled over unseen scrapes, or to grab tufts of wet grass on the steeper slopes. He didn't care or notice.

No sound of thunder reached him, but now and then, far-off sheet lightning illuminated the sky behind Crater Hill, revealing the stark outline of its cone. The lightning spurred Leo on, and not just for its light, which offered only intermittent aid to his progress upward. No, he wanted it to come nearer, to grow wilder, to turn into forked lightning and crack right over Crater Hill, striking at anything on those bare ridges ahead. He could stand out and be a tempting target on that treeless cone up there, and then God might show himself again, this time in a blinding white flash instead of through the rays of the sun. God might help him to escape.

Sometimes people are killed by lightning, Leo knew that, and bare places like this hill were amongst the best places for it. He paused for a moment to think about it before stumbling on up the steeper slope. It seemed to take a long while before he felt the wind freshen and the drops of rain sting his face, signs that he was nearing the exposed ground along the ridge. Not until he felt the slope flatten out beneath him did he stop to regain his breath. As he dropped to the ground, he looked back. The lights of Manoora were well below him now, a loose twinkling web. He tried tracing the dotted light-paths back from the reserve gate to where he thought the shop might be, if only to see the comforting black distance separating him from it.

No going back now. No going back to Rick. No

going back to his mother. He tried to shut her out, and when she wouldn't go, he scrambled to his feet and ran across the ridge, facing away from all those twinkling reminders of Manoora down there.

A distant flash of lightning gave enough light for him to trace the rim of the hill and the shape of the dark saucer that was the ancient crater. Here was as good as anywhere. He stopped and waited for the lightning to come nearer. Uncaring about the rain or the chilling wind, he let them drain the warmth brought to his cheeks by the scramble to the summit. When a bolt did come, he would stretch up his hands as high as they could reach. That would make him a taller target. That would make it easier for God to take him.

Leo waited a long time standing in the blackness. All feeling left him, and once he had to brace his legs and plant his feet apart to keep from falling. A numbness from the cold now spread upward and inward from the hands and feet until his brain was taken to the edge of darkness. Was this the way it was to be? No bolt of lightning at the end of God's pointed limbs, no face, no beckoning greeting, just a numbness and a dark, as dark as the crater's bowl?

'Giving up the ghost' — where did he remember hearing that? He had heard it more than once. It came from the Bible, and it could be something to do with how he felt now. If God didn't come soon, then Leo might give up the ghost without him. Leo didn't want that.

The sheet lightning became less frequent. An odd break fleetingly appeared in the cloud cover, and though the wind kept up cold gusts, the rain became intermittent. Leo didn't notice the changes. It was the sudden appearance of the moon that stirred him. The pointed features of the God he had hoped to see didn't beckon him from the sky. This light fell on him as coldly as the lightning, but softly, evenly.

The Man in the Moon was no God. Its face of craters briefly showed itself, mocked him, and then disappeared again. It wasn't fair; there wouldn't be any God now. The storm had passed. No God.

Numb as he was, Leo's mind gradually sorted that out, and stirred his rigid body. All right then, God could have Crater Hill all to himself if he wanted it! If he didn't choose to help Leo, then he could keep it all. But Leo didn't have to go back to the shop, no one could make him do that.

He stopped looking upward, got his legs working, and quit the summit of the hill, the rest of his body barely responding to his will, its shivering the first sign of life returning to it.

Progress up the hill had been stumbling, but going down was more of a pitch and roll. It didn't help his dizziness, but it helped him to become aware of feeling in his legs. He felt them working like real legs rather than stilts, to take him away from the God who hadn't come. He might have tried to run faster but for the darkness. He blundered blindly forward on any course other than that leading down to the street lamp by the gate, and that course plunged him into the cypress trees before he could stop himself. He forced his way through the barrier, ignoring the abrasive twigs and foliage, only to meet another barrier soon after, one not as yielding — the cemetery fence.

He didn't hit it hard, but hard enough to give him a winding from a lower strand of wire, and torn arms and forehead from the top barbed wire as he pitched down. And that's where he stayed for a few aching minutes — on hands and knees, bloodied, and suffering in the stomach from the blow. There was no God about this. If he died now, it would be just because of a common old barbed wire fence. That wouldn't be the way. Better to go on, just anywhere.

When his stomach was bearable again, he flattened himself to the ground, crawled slowly forward under the fence, and not until he was sure he was well clear of the wire did he get to his feet inside the cemetery. The clouds thinned enough to give the moon a chance again, and by its weak, filtered light, Leo picked out the shape of some kind of shelter or shed not far from where he stood. It gave him something to head for, but reaching it wasn't easy when the clouds swept over and the light was taken.

He made the mistake of going straight towards it, only to find that graves littered the way, some with iron railings, which he didn't discover until his feet tripped on the stone surrounds, thrusting his body against the iron to add to his bruising and pain. Others, just flat slabs of stone, lay in wait in the grass to stub his toes and to fling him on to their pitted surfaces. He was forced to thread his way through this maze.

The shadowy structure ahead had changed the

aimlessness of his flight down from Crater Hill into a determined progress towards a goal, his oasis, a resting-place from all the hurt. But when he finally reached it, Leo found no oasis of comfort, just a shelter of lattice and shingle made for those who sought cover from the sun or rain when they came to the cemetery to bury their dead or to visit the grave of a loved-one.

The intense darkness within made him pause before venturing inside. He felt his way around the entrance post and found his thighs pressing against the end of a seat or bench of hard wooden slats. He followed it right round the inside perimeter until he came to the entrance again. He didn't cross the centre space but worked his way back along the bench to a corner, climbed on to the slats and tried to curl up. Now, all his injuries seemed to ache at once. He shivered, more from the thought of cold that the smell of his wet clothing suggested than from its real effect, but neither cold nor pain kept sleep away for long. The last thing he heard was the soughing of the wind through the lattice.

Eleven

'It's all right nipper, don't worry, you've been found.'

Leo had never heard that voice before. He blinked his eyes, but when they wouldn't clear straight away, he tried rubbing them to life. He winced, and gave a sharp cry as the pain made itself known again.

'It's a bit of a nightmare you've been having, isn't it?' said the voice. 'But never mind, you're lucky I heard a cry just like that from down there in Mrs Kinkaid's summerhouse, or you might have stayed jammed up in that corner and become one of me permanents, with nobody any the wiser. It isn't exactly the best place for anyone to sleep now, is it, especially not a kid who's been knocking himself about like you.'

Leo's eyes focused on the face of the speaker — a smiling man with wrinkles, and false teeth that jiggled a bit when he talked. His eyes looked friendly, all screwed up, but friendly. He didn't seem to expect Leo to say anything yet, because he kept on talking to himself as he tucked a shabby but thick coat around Leo.

'Had to carry you up here to the gatehouse, not

that you're very heavy . . .' He noticed Leo eyeing the room.

'Not really a house here you know, more like an office, isn't it? Sorry I had to put you on these old chairs, but there's nothing else here. It's been the same as this ever since I started as cemetery attendant and grave-digger, forty years ago. Don't have much to do these days, though — they use front-end loaders to dig graves now, did you ever think of that? They can make a hole to fit you in a flash. One time, I used to do it all, but a place as small as this town can't afford a full-time man now you know, and not an old has-been like Bill Wyatt — that's me.' He grinned and pointed to himself.

'Oh no, one time the gardens here used to be a picture, but not any more. All they want me to do is to tell 'em what spaces are left just in case the loader starts digging up an old Manoora citizen. Not that they'll ever run out of space here; you'll be under the ground yourself, nipper, before they fill the place up. Manoora's not going to grow that big. No, they don't bury enough people here to keep on a full-time attendant — that's why you were lucky that there's to be a funeral today. Could've been a week before anyone found you, otherwise. Now, I think as soon as they patch up those cuts of yours and get that cough out of your chest, you'll be as right as rain again.'

He wandered across to the only window of the dingy room and peered out. 'Should be here soon, and then you'll be right', he said, more to himself than to Leo.

He turned and looked back at Leo lying exactly

where he had put him across the two chairs. He couldn't be sure that the boy's open eyes meant that he could hear anything said to him. But that didn't stop Bill.

'I must say I'm blessed if I can work out how you came to be camping out in Mrs Kinkaid's summer-house', he went on. 'That's what I've always called that shelter you were in. It's right next to the grave of Mr Giles Kinkaid — never knew him myself, but he must have been a bit of a big-wig in Manoora with a name like that, mustn't he? I've always reckoned that on a hot day, his wife's spirit sits in that summerhouse after visiting his grave. You see, there's no sign of Mrs Kinkaid anywhere in the cemetery, and yet, all the family are out there, the whole bang lot of them — all the kids must have died in one of them epidemics they sometimes had in them days. So, the big mystery is, where is Mrs Kinkaid?

'Well, I reckon she's one of the real spirits about the place, and this is sure the right spot in Manoora for the spirits, you know. I'll be one myself before very long. But I'm glad I found you before you joined them, young fella', he said, patting the coat covering Leo. 'And I'd like to know how you came to get them cuts, and how you got so wet and all. I dried you out as much as I could, and I'd have cleaned up the cuts for you, but you see I don't keep any first-aid gear up here. Anyway, they look as though the hospital ought to deal with 'em.'

For the first time since he had dropped the boy on to the chairs, Bill detected a change in Leo's expression. He stopped his patter for a moment and bent over as if expecting to hear him speak. 'What is it, nipper? What d'you want to tell me? Your name? Is that what you're going to tell me?'

'Spirits', Leo whispered, huskily, 'any spirits?'

Bill picked up the question, but he frowned, expecting a name to be sounded out. 'Did I hear right? Spirits — is that what you're asking about?'

Leo nodded.

'Well now, fancy you asking about spirits after dossing in Mrs Kinkaid's summerhouse. Yes, my lad, of course there are, at least, I reckon there are. Not everywhere mind, but around this place, for sure. If you'd had my job up here for only a quarter of the time I've been at it, then you'd know about spirits.'

'Crater . . . Hill', Leo managed to say.

'Crater Hill?' Bill frowned again.

'Spirits', Leo repeated.

'Oh', said Bill nodding his head and smiling, 'I suppose you're asking if there are spirits on Crater Hill. Well, yes, I've always reckoned that's why they plonked this here cemetery on it. Them first settlers in Manoora must have felt the Hill was a pretty special kind of place.

'And I'll tell you this, I'd be willing to bet that if one of them saucers, all lit up, comes spinning over Manoora, then it'll land right in that crater up there. It'll settle in that hole and fit just like a body in a coffin, if you know what I mean. Might even happen in your time if you live long enough and don't knock yourself about like you've been doing — your Mum will have to build you up a bit, won't she?'

The noise of a vehicle outside interrupted him.

He went to the window and looked out again. 'Yes, it's them', he said, 'so now everything's going to be all right, isn't it? They'll soon get you on your feet again.'

A faint moan from Leo made Bill turn from the window. 'Hey, don't get upset about it', he said, soothingly, 'They'll be easy on you in the hospital. I had me gall stones taken out at the Manoora Hospital, and they look after you like a lord in there, take my word for it.'

Before Bill could tell if his words had comforted the boy at all, he had to answer the knock.

'Now, where's this live body of yours, you old devil?' said the ambulance man at the head of a stretcher.

'A bit different from the usual, eh Bill!' laughed the other man at the rear.

'Yes', nodded Bill, ushering them through, 'this one's got a bit of life left in him, thanks to Mrs Kinkaid'.

'Who's she?' asked one of the men.

'Oh just one of the special spirits around here. We know she's about, don't we nipper?' Bill said, looking down at Leo.

The men grinned to each other behind the old man's back. They removed the coat and lifted Leo on to the stretcher. As they carried him out to the ambulance, Bill walked alongside, chattering away at Leo.

'In a day or two, I'll try and pop in to see how you're getting on, young fella', he was saying as they slid the stretcher through the rear doors of the ambulance, 'then perhaps, we might talk some more about spirits like Mrs Kinkaid, eh?'

The men grinned again and winked about him, but Bill didn't care. He was rewarded with a fleeting smile from the boy.

Twelve

Leo didn't remember much about his arrival at the hospital and what they first did to him there. He had felt hot, and all the voices sounded far off. Once, he thought he heard some arguing about a needle, something about his parents, but when he tried to focus on who was speaking, the voices hushed and stopped.

The first clear voice came a long while after. 'I think he's really waking now, Mrs Farrell', it said. 'Well Leo, how do you feel now?'

His eyelids blinked and blinked again in the white light of the room. It was a shiny, smiling face before him. Half behind it, the rest of the bed stretched away to its iron end where another figure sat, looking intently at him. He knew those dark-rimmed eyes so well.

His mother rose and came up as close to him as the nurse, but on the opposite side of the bed. He couldn't see beyond the screen that closed off his bed, but it seemed that he wouldn't have to face anyone else, not yet, anyway. That was a relief. He waited for more questions to come.

'How do you feel, Leo?' the nurse repeated.

Lying there awake, he had to answer. 'All

right', he said to her, without much feeling.

The nurse took his short answer for shyness. 'Well, your mother will want to talk to you now, so I'll leave you two together', she said, patting and arranging his pillows to make him comfortable, then turning to his mother, she added, 'And if you want anything, just press the bell there'.

His mother sat down on the edge of the bed quite close to him. She waited for them to be alone before making a move to take Leo's hand in hers. Leo let her, but he didn't know where to look.

'Leo.'

His mother's voice was quiet but firm. Soon, the questions would start.

'Leo, look at me.'

Slowly he did as he was asked. She leaned nearer to him.

'Leo, about Rick.'

'He wrecked my dioramas', he said before she got any further.

'I know that, but you — you could make some others.'

How would she know how long they took to make? Anyway, Rick wouldn't let him make any more, not now. If she asked him about coming home, he wouldn't be able to answer her. He wished she hadn't found him at this hospital so soon. If she hadn't been there when he first woke up, then he might have had time to think of somewhere else to go except back to the shop. She would talk about going back to the shop any minute now, Leo was sure of that, and he wouldn't be able to get out of answering, with her looking like that and sitting so close and him lying in the bed.

'Leo, you will be able to make your dioramas again', she went on.

Why did she have to talk about the dioramas?

'If you're worried about what Rick might do with them, then you needn't be — he's gone.'

The word hit Leo.

'How could he be gone?' he said aloud in disbelief.

'He didn't want to stay in the shop here in Manoora, so he's gone back to the city. He didn't want to come up here in the first place, didn't you know that? He likes city shops better.'

'Didn't you want to go back too?'

'Not this time Leo.'

It was hard for Leo to believe, but why should his mother come here and lie about it. She never lied; she always said it was a sin to lie. Lying wasn't in the Ten Commandments, but she said the false witness one was about the same thing, and she believed in the Ten Commandments, so she wouldn't lie.

'Will he come back?' he asked.

'Not now.'

'But, what about the shop?'

'It's my shop Leo, not his.'

'What about all the work?'

'I can manage if I get a little help to give me a rest now and then.'

Leo could see her rushing about again, except she wouldn't be going backwards and forwards answering the bells. Yes, that was it, there was the loud shop-bell and another tinkly sort — that must have been his father ringing. The bells were

96

clear now, but the face wouldn't come back, just that stare.

And he couldn't remember what he thought of Rick when he first moved in to help. He couldn't see his mother lugging those crates around. But she must have done it once. Anyway, Leo did that job himself now.

What if the shop got busy sometimes? Rick was working in it nearly all the time. Now his mother said that she was going to try and do without him. Often, she liked to go and lie down. But if she didn't try to run the Manoora shop, where would she go? Back to the city after Rick?

'I'm going to need your help', Leo', she was saying.

The nurse reappeared and smiled. 'I think he'd better be left to rest again now, Mrs Farrell', she said, 'he's looking a little flushed again'.

Still holding his hand, his mother leant over and kissed him on the forehead, then let go and stood up. 'He'll be well again soon, won't he?' she asked, anxiously.

'Oh yes', said the nurse, 'it's nearly all passed now, just a trace of fever left, and those cuts and bruises weren't serious, but it's lucky for him that someone got him here before the fever took too strong a hold.'

Why do they always say you're lucky to be alive?

Leo wasn't sure about Rick. He had often heard him say that he was going off, but he never did. Who's to say he won't come back again and smash things up? No use asking God to keep him away. God wouldn't come when Leo needed him. He had only showed himself once, and got Leo into trouble. Or was he really there the second time? Invisible, like his mother often told him. She always said God couldn't be seen. She always said he was there when you needed him. Perhaps he had been there and didn't want to take Leo. Perhaps he had sent Rick away instead. That could be it. The old man in the cemetery believed in spirits. He didn't say anything about having to see them to believe in them.

'I'll come again tomorrow if that's all right', his mother's voice cut in.

'Quite all right', said the nurse. 'See, he's dropping off again. That's all he needs now, sleep and rest for a day or two more.'

The voices trailed off. But Leo didn't sleep for a while after they had left him. He kept wondering about God, whether visible or invisible, whether he had the power to send Rick away — questions, questions, until sleep and images took their place. The image of Mrs Kinkaid sitting alone in her summerhouse . . .

Thirteen

'And how are you feeling now, young fella? You look a bit perkier than when I found you in Mrs Kinkaid's summerhouse, eh?' said Bill Wyatt, coming up to the bed and giving the end of it a slap with his cap.

Bill was Leo's fourth visitor that day. The other three still sat around the bed, not much talk left in any of them.

Leo's mother had brought fruit, and found to her relief that Leo's appetite had grown hearty, that all he wanted to do was munch away. She had expected more questions, and had rehearsed more comforting assurances about Rick. But when Leo didn't mention the subject, she kept her own concerns about their future to herself.

Miss Campieri brought Peter Birchell with her. She gave Leo a hobbies book and said she would be pleased to see him back at school.

Peter said, 'Hi, how d'you feel?' then sat silently on the bed and left the rest to the adults.

Three visitors at once was too much for Leo, and every now and then, he buried himself in the hobbies book.

Bill brought them all to life. Leo's mother

introduced herself and thanked him for finding Leo and looking after him.

'You must tell me how I can get in touch with that Mrs Kinkaid', she said, 'I didn't realize you found Leo in someone's house. I was told —'

Bill threw back his head and chuckled, the false teeth doing their dance. 'You were told I found him in the cemetery Missus, and you were told right — Mrs Kinkaid's summerhouse is what I call the little round shelter standing out in the middle of my cemetery, and that's where your nipper was curled up when I found him.'

'Why do you call it that, Mr Wyatt?' asked Peter.

Bill chuckled again. 'I call it after a lady, a lady who must have lived and died right here in Manoora, but someone forgot to give her a proper headstone, so I give her the summerhouse to keep her spirit safe until it finds a home.'

Anna Campieri smiled. 'That's a nice thought', she said.

Peter wasn't satisfied. 'But how do you know that she died in Manoora if there isn't any stone with her name on and when she died and all that stuff?' he asked.

Leo surprised them all by answering before Bill had a chance to open his mouth. 'Her family is buried there, that's why', he said, as though he knew it by heart. 'Mr Giles Kinkaid and their children, five of them. They died all at once when he drove his cart into the flooded river, and hers was the only body they never found. Everyone said she had taken the school teacher for her new husband and run away with him, so they didn't give her a grave, but she really died with Mr Kinkaid and the children, and ever since then, her spirit has hovered over their graves asking for a place beside them. And when it rains like it did when the river flooded and swept them all away, she takes shelter in the summerhouse and sits there weeping.'

Leo finished as abruptly as he had started, and lay back against the pillow. His cheeks remained flushed, but his eyes, which had flashed with alertness as he had told the story, relaxed again; his lips closed to a quiet smile.

It took a few moments for his visitors to recover.

'Gee', said Peter softly as he turned to face Bill at the other end of the bed, 'was it really like that?'

'So she's really a resident ghost, Mr Wyatt?' said Anna.

'Fancy him remembering all that', said Leo's mother.

Bill scratched the back of his neck, then clamped his cap back on, folded his arms, and stood rocking on his heels, grinning down at Leo.

'Well young fella, I wasn't sure whether you was fit enough to listen when I told you about Mrs Kinkaid, but I can see that you must have been more than wide-awake, because you've remembered a few things that I must have forgotten myself, that's for sure.' His eyes twinkled as he cocked his head and winked at Leo.

'Have you really seen a ghost weeping in the summerhouse, Mr Wyatt?' asked Peter.

It took Bill a moment to shape his answer. 'Seen? Really seen? Well, you know, it's not so much seeing as hearing. Yes, that's it, hearing

— hearing the sobs now and then, and sometimes the rustle of her long skirts across the paving stones of the summerhouse as she goes out to ask for her own spot beside the gravestone of her husband and the four little stones of her children.'

'Four?' queried Peter, 'Leo just said that there were five children'.

Bill lifted his cap and scratched his neck again. 'Yes, so he did, so he did. And you know something, he's right, because two of the Kinkaid nippers was twins. See, there's only one headstone for the pair of 'em. You'd know that if I showed you the writing on their stone. They was probably buried side by side. What beats me, is how the nipper here . . .'

He broke off in mid-sentence, frowning, as though he was puzzled by a sudden odd thought. They waited for him to go on, but he didn't. He just stood, scratching his neck and shaking his head.

'We must come up to your cemetery for a visit as a class, mustn't we Peter?' said Anna 'I've never thought of it as a likely place for an excursion, but you've reminded me that sometimes gravestones can tell us quite a lot about the local history of a place like Manoora.'

Peter would have liked to ask Bill what it was that 'beat him' — he could see that the old cemetery attendant was still pondering over it. But before he got the chance, Anna suggested they should leave so that Leo could have the rest of the visiting time alone with his mother. Bill took the hint, and soon after, he too prepared to leave.

'Quite a nipper you've got there', he said to

Leo's mother as he shook her hand warmly.

Though Leo wouldn't have minded them all staying longer, he couldn't get the words out to ask them.

Bill gave the bed a parting flick with his cap. 'Five — beats me how you could've known', he muttered.

Leo didn't have words for that either.

At the door Bill swung round. 'Quite a nipper', he repeated, shaking his head.

Reassured by their visit, Leo's mother talked out her relief when she and Leo were left together again. 'You see, they are friendly to you, all of them, your teacher, and that boy Peter she brought along, he'll be a friend to you at school, and old Mr Wyatt, he likes you. Wasn't it kind of him to come and visit, he didn't have to do that. None of them is going to hold it against you, Leo.'

Leo was lying back against the pillows, hands clasped behind his head, his gaze more vacant than attentive, his smile more a response to some thought from within than to what she was saying.

'Leo, are you listening? I was saying you don't have to worry about everyone here remembering what you did to that sheep.'

'Oh, that', was all Leo said in reply, his smile fading briefly before his mind took him elsewhere.

Fourteen

'Can you see him?' called Woodoh.

'Yep', answered Carl, doing a monkey act out amongst the greenery at the end of the branch.

'What's he doing?'

'He's still up near the top. He's sitting on his tractor, talking to someone.'

'Keep your eye on him for a minute, and if he stays up there, come back and have your half.'

It was good to be perched up in the cypress again. Woodoh and Carl had steered clear of Crater Hill since their visit to Baldy Braithwaite. They'd played down by the river mostly, but the hill was better for bike races and climbing. Peter wasn't with them as much these days, but he tagged along this day when they urged him to join them. Races down the drive from Crater were much better with three than two, Woodoh had said.

Seeing Baldy out on his tractor up on the hill had forced them to abandon their bikes for a while and settle for climbing instead. Half-way up the giant tree, Peter had propped, jammed himself against the main trunk, then pulled out from his pocket a chocolate bar, and begun chewing.

The smell of it must have reached the other two just above him, because they halted their climb, asked what he was doing, then dropped back to join him.

Woodoh sent Carl out along the branch to reconnoitre first, while he started on the chocolate that Peter had given them to share.

'Haven't seen this sort before, where'd you get it?' asked Woodoh.

'Mrs Farrell gave it to me.'

'Why'd she do that?'

'I was there this morning working in the shop. Been there a couple of other times too.'

'D'you get paid for it?' asked Carl, rejoining them and claiming his share of the chocolate from Woodoh.

'Course, but she gives me drinks and things as well.'

'Doesn't looney Leo do anything?'

'Yeah, he does a lot. And he's not too looney, either', Peter added.

'He's a bit weird though, you'd have to admit', said Woodoh.

'Yeah, I mean who ever heard of anyone knocking off a sheep like that?' said Carl.

'That was weeks ago', said Peter.

'Oh come off it, he's not likely to change in that time, is he?' said Carl.

Peter shrugged. 'Maybe not, but Miss Campieri reckons he's all right.'

'She's soft though', said Woodoh.

'Reynoldsy would be different, don't you reckon, Woodoh?' laughed Carl.

'I'll say', he agreed, 'you kids in her grade don't

know when you're well off. Reynolds isn't as bad as old Frenchy, but he's bad enough.'

'Well Frenchy thinks Farrell's all right now, too', said Peter.

'You're joking!' laughed Woodoh.

'Nup. Miss Campieri got the Head to come down and look at one of Leo's dioramas that he brought to show our grade.'

'His what?' Carl frowned.

'Dioramas.'

'What are they?' asked Woodoh.

'They're sort of models of scenes, only all set up inside a box with a spy-hole at one end for you to look through, and then there are more holes cut in the lid and covered with coloured cellophane to let the light in, and when you look inside, all the trees and people and things look fantastic with the coloured light on them. Even old Frenchy thought it was great.'

'Still sounds a bit kooky to me', said Carl.

The sound of Braithwaite's tractor interrupted them. 'You hear that', said Woodoh, 'he's getting closer. Hop out and see what old Baldy's doing. I'm going higher.'

Peter stayed where he was while the other two went their different ways.

Carl was the first to report. 'He's coming down the drive a bit, but he's stopped again to talk to some other people — he's always checking up on everyone. Whose park is it anyway? You'd think he owned it.'

From above, Woodoh let out a happy squawk as he swung out on to a branch.

'Hey, shut up Woodoh, he might hear you from

where he is', called Carl.

'Don't be a nut', he replied, 'he couldn't hear me above that rattly old heap of a tractor. Hey, Birchell!'

'What?'

'Just after we've been talking about your mate Leo, I can see him now, down in the cemetery. Old Bill Wyatt's with him, and they're near that little shed thing. Go out on the end of your branch, and you'll see.'

'Why?'

'Because you might be able to work out what he's doing in there.'

Peter crawled gingerly along the branch and tried to part the greenery. It opened enough for him to see a small section of the cemetery, but not the part near the summerhouse. He drew back along the branch to a safer perch.

'I couldn't see them from out there', he called.

'Well I'll tell you what they're doing, and see if you can make any sense out of it', said Woodoh. 'The kid is holding a kind of cross steady while old Bill is hammering it into the ground. I think it must be made of wood. And now they've stopped and they're standing back looking at it. And now . . . and now Leo has gone over to a grave near it and he's picking some flowers. He's taking them back and putting them up against the wooden cross thing. Old Bill's gone over to the little shed. He's waving to Leo — the kid's going over and they've both gone inside . . .

'Gee, they weren't long in there. Here they are out again, and old Bill's doing a sort of dance. He's shaking Leo's hand, and now he's putting his hand on Leo's shoulder and they're walking away towards the gatehouse . . . they've gone out of my sight now. I'm coming down.'

The diorama that Leo had made leapt back into Peter's mind — the summerhouse and the graves standing on the bottom of the box, and the cottonwool all wispy, stuck on twigs to look like mist in the trees, and the figure of Mrs Kinkaid hanging from the fine wires as if she was floating in air or something, above the graves of the family, and when you held the diorama under a lamp, she would swing in and out of the light shining down through the blue cellophane covering one big round hole in the top just like a moon, and it all looked . . .

'Hey, did you hear all that, Carl?' said Woodoh as he reached their level.

Carl shuffled back a little way from his spying spot. 'Some of it. What's it all about?' he asked.

'Haven't a clue, but old Bill Wyatt and Leo Farrell must be mates.'

'He's a bit of an old kook himself, I reckon', said Carl.

'What d'you make of it, Peter?' asked Woodoh.

'They gave Mrs Kinkaid a grave.'

'What? What are you talking about?'

'They're helping Mrs Kinkaid's spirit to rest.'

'Sounds crackers to me', said Woodoh.

'Me too', Carl agreed.

'It was all in his diorama', said Peter.

'Oh, not those things again', said Carl. He wasn't interested in this kind of talk, and scrambled back along his branch to his spying spot.

'D'you believe in all that spirit stuff too?' asked Woodoh.

Peter shrugged, 'I dunno, but . . .'

'Hey!' called Carl, 'Baldy's coming down the drive.'

'Well shut up then and stop shaking that branch, you idiot!' ordered Woodoh.

They waited, listening to the approaching pop-pop of Braithwaite's tractor. It seemed to be nearly under them when it stopped and the engine cut. The three looked at each other and kept silent.

Baldy's big voice boomed up from below. 'I know you're up there somewhere, so get down good and quick!'

'How would he know we're here?' whispered Woodoh.

Braithwaite couldn't have heard him, but it seemed as if he must have picked up the whisper when he yelled, 'Your bike gave you away, so don't think I'm not awake up to where you are!'

It didn't sound like bluffing.

'Whose bike?' whispered Carl angrily at the other two.

'Yes, whose?' said Woodoh.

They both turned to Peter.

'You came up a bit after us, didn't you?' Carl accused. 'Didn't you put your bike out of sight by the cemetery fence?'

Baldy's voice boomed again. 'All right then, I'll be confiscating this bike, and that will be the last you'll see of it!'

Without saying anything, Peter began to climb down.

'Hey!' called Woodoh in a hoarse whisper, 'what are you doing?'

Peter looked back up at them. He couldn't be bothered playing the game any more. 'I'm going down, you don't have to come', he said.

'But . . .' Carl began to protest.

'Don't worry, I won't tell him you were up here too.'

And he didn't look back. They watched him disappear awkwardly under the web of branches, snapping off a couple of dead sticks almost as though he wanted to let old Braithwaite know he was coming. They grinned to each other and shook their heads.

Peter didn't feel much like grinning when he emerged from the lower branches and dropped to the grass. Everything always looked bigger after being up high, and Braithwaite standing beside his tractor looked big enough to swallow him.

'I thought it'd be one of you lot', he said. 'What about your mates. Where are they?'

It was worth a try. 'What mates?' said Peter.

Braithwaite dropped the bike and advanced a step or two nearer. Peter backed away, instinctively.

'That Woodmason, and that other log with the blond mop, what's his name?'

'Forster.'

'Yeah, that's him, aren't they your mates?'

Peter couldn't see any way out. 'Yep', he admitted.

'Well where are they then, still up there?'

'They're in the reserve somewhere, but I can't say for sure exactly where', said Peter.

It was the best he could do for Woodoh and Carl. If Braithwaite went on, then he'd wring the truth out of him soon enough. But lucky for Peter, Braithwaite was more interested in getting down to his house for afternoon tea than wasting time looking for any more kids up in trees. He turned, picked up Peter's bike and tossed it into the trailer.

'I'll be keeping this for a week. You can walk home, and let it be a lesson to you. And you can tell your mates that I'll be nabbing their bikes too if I catch up with them.'

He started the motor, and drove away towards the entrance gates. Peter followed on foot in the same direction, positive that Braithwaite would be looking at him in his mirrors. He kept walking until the tractor went out through the gates, turned towards Braithwaite's house, and then disappeared from sight.

Peter stopped, swung round, and looked back up at the cypresses. He stood quite still for a moment, thinking. Then slowly, he started walking again, but not towards the main gates this time. He headed for the cemetery fence.

If he was lucky, he might catch up with Leo at the gatehouse.

about the author

Ted Greenwood was born in Melbourne in 1930. For some years he worked as a school teacher and then in 1959 he graduated from RMIT in Fine Art (Painting) and became a lecturer in Art and Craft at Toorak State College. In 1968 he gave up his lecturing to devote time to writing and illustrating children's books.

Five of his books for children have won awards and in 1972 he was given a Churchill Fellowship to travel to places of book and art interest, and to meet children in a variety of situations. Four of his books are published by Penguin: *Ginnie* (Kestrel), *V.I.P.* (Picture Puffin), *The Pochetto Coat* and *The Boy who saw God* (both in Puffin).

Ted Greenwood lives in the Dandenong Ranges in Victoria.

The Pigman's Legacy
Paul Zindel

Consumed with guilt and grief since the death of Mr Pignati, John and Lorraine determine to help another old man they find in his abandoned house. They force their way into his life, full of plans to make amends for their past mistakes, but things go very wrong and they begin to wonder if the Pigman's legacy is simply too much for them to handle.

Displaced Person
Lee Harding

Life is ordinary for seventeen-year-old Graeme Drury until, inexplicably, people start to ignore him. Gradually, his world slips away from him; and it becomes grey, silent and insubstantial. Graeme has to question what is real. Even his girl Annette, becomes a ghost. Alone he must come to terms with a new existence, moving in a dream that is horrifyingly true.

Empty World
John Christopher

Neil Miller is alone after the death of his family in an accident. So when a virulent plague sweeps across the world, dealing death to all it touches, Neil has a double battle for survival: not just for the physical necessities of life, but with the subtle pressures of fear and loneliness.

Tulku
Peter Dickinson

Escape from massacre, journey through bandit lands, encounters with strange Tibetan powers – and beneath the adventures are layers of idea and insight. Winner of both the Carnegie and Whitbread Awards for 1979.

Survival
Russell Evans

High tension adventure of a Russian political prisoner on the run in the midst of an Arctic winter.

Mischling, Second Degree
Ilse Koehn

Ilse was a Mischling, a child of mixed race – a dangerous birthright in Nazi Germany. The perils of an outsider in the Hitler Youth and in girls' military camps make this a vivid and fascinating true story.

A Long Way To Go
Marjorie Darke

The fighting rages in France, and posters all over London demand that young men should join up. But Luke has other feelings - feelings that are bound to bring great trouble on him and the family. Because nobody has much sympathy for a conscientious objector – perhaps the only answer is to go on the run.